52 Weeks to Exceptional Leadership

by Kim Nugent

52 Weeks to Exceptional Leadership

Publisher: Sojourn Publishing

Paperback ISBN: 978-1-62747-174-9
Hardcover ISBN: 978-1-62747-172-5
EBook: 978-1-62747-176-3

For further information, please contact Kim Nugent at kim@drnugentspeaks.com or www.drnugentspeaks.com for information on how to book Dr. Nugent for speaking and training engagements for your next event.

Personal Branding Expert: Gagan Sarkaria, Unfold Your Success.

Cover Designer: Gagan Sarkaria & Abbey Wilkerson | www.UnfoldYourSuccess.com

Author Photo: Munaza Saiyed | www.UnfoldYourSuccess.com

Dedication

To Kelly, Stacey, Tanya, Esmeralda, Bridgette, and Stephanie, the best leaders I ever had the privilege to work with on a daily basis. Thank you to the Executive Committee and all the employees at the university who made my life a joy every day. Finally, a special thank-you to my supervisor, Mark, who supported us to do our best.

Table of Contents

Foreword

The intention of this book is for you, the reader, to address one strategy per week for one year. Once you implement each strategy, make notes in the provided journal space about what worked and what could be improved. This weekly practice will become a habit. My goal is to provide fifty-two strategies to build a strong foundation for your leadership development. This is a practical guide to build on the special skills and talents you bring to the position.

While you can certainly read topics in random order, based on your immediate priorities and concerns, try not to read the whole book and just put it away. If your preferred learning style is to read the whole book for the framework, context, and content, that is fine. But make sure to go back and reread one strategy a week and complete each journal page to further reflect on your implementation of the strategy with your team. This is the true value of the book.

Introduction

Leaders and managers who have the responsibility for developing talent, this book is for you. While you will use your company resources and your own experience, this book can be a weekly guide for the first year. It can provide a real structure to build upon. It can save you time and money and give you a topic for your weekly coaching calls or meetings.

Did you know there are more than 57,600 books on leadership listed on Amazon, and the list continues to grow? Because I am always looking for ways to improve my leadership abilities and coaching skills and to challenge my thinking, I have read many of these books throughout the years and continue to do so.

So why would you bother to actually purchase another book? A true leader never stops learning and growing, and seeks out new resources to bring to the team. Examples include books, podcasts, speakers, short courses, degree programs, and much more. If we stay only in our current operating state of what we know, we will never grow or stretch ourselves or our thinking.

The reality is that employees are being promoted everyday into management and leadership positions. According to Character, Drivers and Rewards Leadership (CDR) Assessments, 50 percent to 75 percent of the people in leadership positions are ineffective or underqualified. Budgets to train and develop managers and leaders are shrinking, so it falls to you. The future of leadership is your responsibility. So, now what?

First, you must model what you want and the culture you are striving to create. Everything you do should align with and reflect the mission of the organization. You must know what goals you want to achieve and create a pathway for achieving those goals. You must build an organization of trust and integrity. You must listen to your stakeholders.

The second part of the process is hiring the best person for the position in terms of soft skills, background, and ability. So if the development role falls to you, this book is for you. This book was written based on my years of experience, trial and error, the courses I took, books, nationally known speakers' comments, mentors, and common sense. It is a practical approach and tool to help new managers and leaders navigate the new role and build upon the skills they currently possess.

This book provides new leaders with practical ideas to build skills, such as communication, collaboration, creativity, operations, talent development, time management, and accountability. We know every supervisor can provide vision, orientation, strategy, and annual plans, but how can you insure improvement week by week?

One of the more effective development strategies I have used is to purchase a book as a guide to help frame my weekly coaching conversations with each new leader I train. I buy a current book for myself and a copy for the new leader. Then through a guided weekly discussion, I discuss each strategy in detail and how it can be used week by week.

If you are a new leader, I recommend that you read one strategy weekly, then implement, reflect, and discuss how it can improve the overall operation. By using this book, you can create a culture of accountability. A reflection page follows each strategy. The overall goal is to improve your organization.

Preface

It was Thursday, April 23, 2015, the worst day of my professional life. As a university administrator, it was my role to call a town-hall meeting for the three company locations in Houston. It was my responsibility to inform my entire colleague base that everyone would be losing their jobs over the next eighteen months. A corporate decision had been made to transition our on-ground campus locations to online only. This would require a great deal of coordination and communication. After the university announcements, the group vice president, the regional Human Resources manager, and I met with every department to help answer questions.

I am most proud of our company for providing, within twenty-four hours of the meeting, a package of information to each employee that included the estimated stay-through date of his or her employment. This helped alleviate our employees' uncertainty, or at least as much as we could predict at that point. We then met individually with anyone who wanted to sit and discuss their personal situation. To say everyone was in shock was an understatement.

My immediate attention was on the Admissions department, because their stay-through date was only three weeks away. Our company was great in providing an outsourcing company called Right Management Services. The employees could use these outsourcing career services once they lost their jobs, but that did not help the Admissions staff in the meantime. Since we were no longer enrolling, what were they supposed to do?

I requested home-office support to send a career-services professional to come and work with our soon-to-be-laid-off employees as well as the rest of the colleagues who wanted help. The company sent a senior career-service staff member, and she worked tirelessly for three days with employees. She helped update resumes, update their LinkedIn profiles, conduct some mock interviews, review O*NET online services for career exploration and job analysis, and determine next steps. She was exceptional. In addition, our own Career Services team helped support employees throughout the eighteen months.

In the meantime, I went to work networking with other schools to help transition our employees where possible. The Executive Committee members were great in helping us identify where employees wanted to go next and how we could help them. Each week, I sent out possible job leads for employees based on their end date, working through each group. My managers did the same. Our goal was to make this transition as seamless as possible.

We still had a university to operate. We could not afford to have our students think we would abandon them, and we did not. My constant message to our Executive Committee was that it was business as usual. We all knew it was not, but we had to create that mindset. On the operational side, the managers and employees had to function each day as if things were normal–and they did. It was a bit strange. On one hand, as an employee with a later stay-through date, one has a job to do: take care of the students, focus on the job at hand, and be happy to have a paycheck. On the other hand, it was natural to think, *What if I do not find a job, and there is no new paycheck on the date I am supposed to leave the university?* This was particularly hard for employees who might have a stay-through date of six months or a year. Truthfully, we did not discourage them from looking for new jobs. We allowed them to take time off, schedule phone interviews while at work, and go to interviews. Everyone was going through the same thing. We also said if you get an offer, take it if it is right for you, but don't panic and take just any job. You have time, so make sure it is right for you. We will figure out how to deal with it operationally and fill positions that might be open sooner than planned.

Next, we brought in three different teaching organizations for our staff members, to explain how to go about obtaining a Texas teaching certificate if that is where their heart led them. We never stopped trying to assist in the transition.

The managers had to work out individual student degree plans (called "teach-out" plans), class by class, one student at a time. The work was tedious but necessary. We had to work out partnership agreements with other colleges and universities. We made sure each student had an opportunity to stay for the eighteen months our institution would be open, or transition and be able to graduate. We held student town-hall meetings every day for the first week, sent out numerous emails, and talked to faculty so they had the correct information to help students get to the right person to answer their questions. Once the students' shock wore off, they became concerned for each faculty and staff member. It was heartfelt concern, and everyone appreciated the students even more. I think you can tell from the description: it was truly a special place.

While the news was personally and professionally devastating for everyone working at the three Houston locations, I have never worked with a better group of professionals. Our employees stayed. There was no mass exodus from our students. The students wanted to stay and graduate.

As an executive committee, we decided to be the model for our company on how to handle a transition and teach-out in the most positive and professional way possible. It was a humbling experience. Everyone on my team was on board. No matter how stressful the days were, my team never showed it. I miss them all. As I have said before, it was a very special place.

Fast forward twenty-two months, and the transition is complete. I check on my managers and employees every so often either by text, phone, Facebook, or having lunch. It's great to reconnect. The conversations go something like this: "I like where I work, the job I am doing, and the people I work with, but it is not the same work environment we had when we worked for you, Kim." At first, I thought, *What gracious feedback,* and started to dismiss it as just colleagues being kind. I really did not think I did anything unique. Then I recently attended a leadership workshop put on by Character, Drivers, and Rewards (CDR) Assessments and found that the research states that 50 percent to 75 percent of leaders are ineffective. So the conclusion is that what I did was effective, and I want to pass it on to improve leadership development for others. The purpose of the book is twofold. First, it can help you, the reader, become a better manager. Second, it can help you become a better trainer of managers.

The First Thirty Days on the Job

New Bosses Should Come with Warning Labels

If you have worked for the same company for a few years, you've probably had the experience of a change in management. Change is emotional for most people. It causes uncertainty. Sometimes, the employees are excited. Sometimes, the employees are concerned. Employees wonder about the leadership style of the new person in charge.

Employees' initial thoughts always come down to *What does it mean to me? How will my life be affected? Do I still have a job? Will I be asked to do more with less resources or pay? What other changes will happen? What are the new leader's expectations?*

For the leader, the emotions are similar but different from that of an employee. For the new leader, there is certainly excitement about the new situation, and yet the leader has a specific charge. At this point, the leader already has a sense of the culture of the organization, the team, possibly the board of directors, the issues, and the immediate challenges to be solved. Merely having a sense of the organization is not enough, though. Until you get to know the team, listen and ask questions. Having only "a sense" is a trap.

As for me, I have changed roles inside organizations and held many leadership roles in several organizations. What I have discovered is that even if the change in leadership will improve the organization in the long run, employees have no idea who the new manager is in terms of personality, management style, or what they believe in. This takes time. Often, this is time the leader does not have.

Most helpful is to hold a company meeting (face to face if possible, depending on the size of the organization) in the first week. Technology can be used for remote locations for the initial introduction, so everyone feels included. The message must be authentic, including how you feel, what you value about the organization, and what you want from the employees. The message should start with what *is not* changing, such as the mission, vision, and values–things employees can hold on to and then listen to what *is* changing.

I always included three points that are important to me when I worked at the university level. My expectations are:

- **Do the Right Thing:** No matter what, do the right thing. Do what is best in the situation for the student, faculty member, staff member, or the employer. I say that we will not second-guess you. If you make a mistake, we will discuss it so we can all learn from it.
- **No Surprises:** Never surprise us. If you make a mistake or there is a problem, let us know immediately. We can work through the issue together. We are all human, and mistakes will happen. We are a learning organization.
- **The Elevators:** Talk with students or employees when in the elevator, cafeteria, student lounge, or the hallways. In the elevator, the students and employees are a captive audience. Most people are quiet in an elevator, and this is a great opportunity to just see how each person is doing. I have always felt if we ask a student, "How are you?" and the student says, "Okay," we have an opportunity to ask a few more questions. Something might be "off" for the student at school or home. The student(s) should say "Great" or "Well." My experience tells me that for most students, the university is a sanctuary. A place of focus and caring. A place to have friends. A place to study an area of interest, learn, and grow. So when the response is just "Okay," something is going on with that student. We show we care about their well-being and help.

I conclude my initial conversation with my new employees by saying that over time, we will all get to know each other, and I look forward to the conversations. I open the meeting for questions or concerns. I then let them know how I plan on getting to know them. This investment of time will create a strong foundation on which to build. Cultivating relationships is key to cultivating a strong culture, accomplishing the mission and goals of any organization, and building trust.

"I am not the last of old bosses. I am the first of new leaders." –Richard Daley, American politician

The First Days on the Job as the Leader

My perspective has changed over the years on how I should spend my first thirty days on the job. When I was a young manager, I thought I had to hit the ground running and make an immediate impact or change. While some of those situations did require swift action, my approach would be different today. In those days, I would have gone in and made swift staff changes, restructured, brought in new people, and made immediate changes.

I do not operate that way today. With experience, I have learned the best thing to do in the first thirty days is to listen and observe. Initially, I set up a meeting with each Executive Committee member and get to know them. After these meetings, I met with each manager and then employees in small groups or one on one. In addition, when I was at the university, I met with every full-time faculty member. What was the point in doing this? I felt I needed to understand the culture. I needed to understand what each person loved about working for the company. I asked what the employees saw as the challenges or weaknesses. It gave me time to get to know them individually. It helped me learn about the talents and strengths of the organization. As a result, I appreciated their years of experience, their passion, and the effort they had given to the organization. Is that all I did during the first thirty days? No, of course not, but I listened, I learned, I began to build trust. The investment of this time is priceless. In addition, if you have remote locations, it is critical to include them in visits and these types of conversations. When you make the effort of investing time in people, the benefits are tenfold. You may think you do not have the time, but quite frankly, if you do not make the time, you will waste time, energy, and resources.

The point is to avoid the simple mistakes I have seen other leaders make. I have personally seen new managers come into an organization, not appreciate the culture, and not take the time to get to know the people who built the organization. The consequences were always disastrous for the person—and the organization.

"We need to learn to observe and listen to people and get to know them."—Corey Johnson, American actor

So You Think You Know Talent? Hiring the Right Candidate

Have you ever hired someone and suddenly realized you had made a mistake and the person was not a good fit? Did you think back through what happened or what could be learned? Did you just go with your gut? Did you miss all the signs? I know most of us have. I want to share what I have learned over the years that has helped me.

First, before you post the job opening, make sure the job description is up-to-date. That is critical to avoiding problems later. Once the resumes have been reviewed, determine which candidates will be asked to interview. Make sure the candidate actually possesses the educational background you require before contacting the employee. I cannot tell you how many people make this mistake. In the case of hiring for a position that requires specific academic credentials, have the applicants send you unofficial copies of their transcript in advance. It is actually surprising how many people think the name of their degree is a match for the job, but upon further examination of their transcript, it becomes clear that it is not. Also, if you are interviewing for a teaching or training position, build in a mock presentation as part of the interview process.

At a minimum, hold at least three interviews with the candidate. These may be a combination of phone, face-to-face, or Skype, individual, or group interviews. Why three? Candidates can always be at their best for one interview, but can they sustain it? You need to see the candidate at different times of the day, interviewed by different people.

Make sure everyone, including the candidate, has a copy of the current job description. This will help focus everyone on what is required. We know most candidates are not a 100 percent match. Find out where the gaps are, so you can decide if training can help or if the gaps are too great and there is no match after all.

Have a set of behavioral, situational, and job-related questions. Make sure the interviewer has the questions in advance and a rating sheet so the most objective decision can be made. Prior to the interviews, make sure everyone on the interviewing team knows the expectations and their roles. Without this preparation, interviews can go badly. The interview has two outcomes. First, you are trying to find the right candidate. Second, the candidate is trying to determine if this position at this company is a good fit. Without the interviewers' preparation, I have found individuals make it tough on the potential candidate and ruin it for the company. So you have to invest time up front to make the process work.

Finally, I believe you have to ask yourself, *Can I work with this person? Is this person going to elevate and improve our operation? Does this candidate bring a unique skill set we are lacking and need?* These may not be typical Human Resources questions, but they seem to work for me. Check references and conduct a background check for both external and internal candidates. This is especially important if the candidate currently works for the same organization for which you are hiring. Too many times, a hiring manager assumes that the candidate is good because they work or worked for the same organization. Contact the supervisor and find out. You cannot afford a surprise here.

My intention was to always "hire up" from the skill set of the previous candidate in the role. Our world changes so fast, and we cannot remain at the same level. Hire up and do not be threatened that the candidate knows more than you. You cannot know everything.

"The harder you work, the luckier you get."–Plato, classical Greek philosopher

Hired. Now, What?

So the interview team concluded their work, and the offer has been made and accepted by the candidate. I have seen many teams high-five themselves and then go back to work, forgetting about the fact that now the real preparation starts.

Are you ready for the new hire? Where will they sit? Is this an office-based position? Is this a remote position?

What equipment is needed? Computer, printer, remote-access connection, applications, phone extension, email address, keys, etc. Has the equipment been tested to make sure it is ready?

What other supplies are needed? Name plates for the cubicle or office door, office supplies, business cards, etc. In this age of fast printing services, you can have those business cards ready by the time the new hire starts. What kind of impression does it make on a new employee to have everything set up?

Did the new hire receive a welcome letter letting him or her know the exact start date, time, and location of the first day? Has the employee orientation date and time been set up? Can some of the normal Human Resources paperwork be transmitted electronically prior to the start date to save time? Have you told the new hire what to bring on the first day, if anything? Did you send him a small welcome gift with the company logo? Did you plan to take her and/or the team to lunch on the first day? Did you check in with the new employee at the end of the first day to see how he or she is doing? Did you check in at the end of the week to do the same? Take nothing for granted. Do the same thing after thirty days.

Making a good first impression is all in the details. I have heard some managers tell me they do not order business cards before the employee arrives, because what happens if they do not show? Seriously? I would rather spend $20.00 to have cards on their desk so they know we are eager to have them on board.

Develop a new-hire checklist to make sure you have everything to create a good first impression. Employees make their decision about whether they have made a good decision about working for an organization within the first few days.

Once you feel you have perfected the process, ask the employee whether they need anything you did not provide. You will find you continue to perfect your new-hire checklist. Good luck onboarding!

"If you hire people just because they can do a job, they'll work for your money. But if you hire people who believe what you believe, they'll work for you with blood, sweat, and tears."
–Simon Sinek, British/American author, motivational speaker, and marketing consultant

Do You Want the Good News or the Bad News First? Setting Expectations

Have you ever become frustrated that your employees are not living up to your expectations? If you answered yes, I might have some bad news. Take responsibility for the expectations you are setting, before you blame the employees.

Here are some examples:

1. An employee coming in late to work
2. A participant late to a conference call or a meeting
3. A direct report not being prepared for a meeting
4. Expense reports arriving late
5. Staff taking too long to respond to phone calls and emails

Example One:

Coming in late is an interesting problem. New supervisors sometimes have a tendency to overlook it until one day it becomes a crisis. Then the supervisor is angry and takes it out on the employee. The employee wonders what the issue was since you never addressed it all the times before–why is today such a big deal? Think about it. You allowed the situation to happen. You have conflicting expectations. My advice is to address it immediately by asking, "What happened?" Depending on the response, remind them when they are supposed to be at work. This is especially important if the person's position is critical to the operation or is reliant upon client interaction.

There are also positions in a company where it is not critical that employees have to be in at a specific time, yet the work product must be accomplished. For some people, flex hours may be the solution. Management is not a one-size-fits-all approach. My recommendation is to be fair and consistent.

Example Two:

So, what do you do when an employee is late to a call or meeting? Do you start the call or meeting on time? Or do you wait for everyone to arrive? Have you ever considered how disrespectful it is to those employees who arrived to the meeting on time to have to sit and wait? This costs money and can be frustrating to the employees. It sends the message to not bother showing up on time, because the supervisor will wait. Equally important is to end the meeting on time, because participants may have to go back to work or go to another meeting or make a call. My recommendation is to respect their time as much as you want your time respected.

Example Three:

Have you ever expected someone on your team to be ready to report on the progress of an initiative, and they weren't ready? Think about the last meeting you held with this person, whether in a group or one on one. Did you clarify when the employee should be ready with a status update? Do you do that consistently in group meetings and one-on-one coaching meetings with all employees? Or do you leave it open-ended for them to guess? Do you hold them accountable? Do you model this? What is your strategy for solving this problem?

Example Four:

It is extremely frustrating when an employee turns in an expense report after the month-end close. How can you keep this from happening? Explain the importance of recording the expense in the month it was incurred. Teach them a strategy to help them remember. I found myself early in my career getting into a habit that has helped me. Every Friday, I completed my expense report and turned it in before I left the office, no matter what time. I did not have to worry about missing a deadline and being stressed about it. My recommendation is to send an email reminder a few days before month end. It will help build a new habit, reduce frustration, and achieve timely expense submissions.

Example Five:

Poor response time on emails and returned phone calls can happen with both employees and managers. First, does your company have a set expectation? My recommendation is to create one if your company does not have such a policy. For example, emails and phone calls should be responded to within twenty-four hours during the week and seventy-two hours over the weekend. I worked for a Fortune 100 company, and this policy was in place. Once new employees and managers were held to the expectation, it worked.

As a leader or manager, you must model the behavior. Set the expectations and teach them how to meet those expectations. Don't *assume* anything.

"Expectations determine outcome, always!"—Deepak Chopra, Indian-American physician, public speaker, and writer

The Honeymoon is Over

You just got hired for a new job, and you are so excited. It is your first day, and lots of things are happening. You go to orientation, have a tour, and find your work area all set up with supplies, phone lists, business cards, and a nameplate. You meet the team and begin to read policies and procedures, all before lunch. You go to lunch with your manager. Things seem to be going well. In the afternoon, you get access to your company email and the password to the portal, and you start your department orientation. You have met more people than you can remember, and it seems like you are a good fit. It seems like they knew you were coming and welcomed you. It was a flawless first day.

After about the third day, you know where you are going and are remembering people's names. Then after about two weeks, things begin to shift. What you thought you would be doing is not exactly as described in the job description or in the interviews. It seems like there is a new weight on the job description, or importance to miscellaneous duties as required, or whatever the manager decides he or she wants you to do that day.

Thirty days go by, and it seems like you are in a mediocre state. You are not exactly excited like the first day, but not exactly ready to quit. You are just dealing with the day-to-day work. Over the next sixty days, you feel this is not the job you signed on for. It is not what you were told. This is the beginning of a feeling that the honeymoon is over. Real work life begins.

Generally, for employees, the honeymoon lasts six weeks to ninety days. As a manager, this is a critical time for you to recognize what employees go through, regardless of level or title. It is critical that you set up a meeting with all new hires sixty days after they start; don't wait until ninety days, as it is too late. Put it on your calendar. Hold an afternoon coffee-and-cookie meeting, ice-cream break, or lunch meeting, depending on the number of new hires. As the leader of the organization, do not delegate this–invite them personally. I held these meetings six times a year. I sent out invitations calling it "Food for

Thought." Explain that their feedback is critical to improving the operation, and tell them how you will use their feedback.

Simply ask the following questions:

- What do you like about working here?
- What can be improved? (Be specific, and let us know what bothers you or frustrates you.)
- What surprised you?

Take notes. My experience was that after two years of consistently holding these meetings, we had improved the operation significantly, so much so that new employees had a difficult time coming up with new ways to help us improve. We did not stop holding the meetings. New employees are your gift of new insights and ways of operating differently. Listen carefully, and keep the honeymoon going.

Strive to celebrate many, many more happy anniversaries.

"Every accomplishment begins with the decision to try."—Anonymous

Communication

The Rule of Three Emails

Isn't technology great? Remember life before emails and texts? There were face-to-face conversations. There were phone calls. Technology provides new options. Now we can quickly expedite communication, locally and globally. We can hit the Enter key and think we are awesome. We can think we are productive. We can think we are communicating well.

Think again.

Have you ever sent out an email and received a response that seemed confusing, upsetting, or incomplete? The answer is probably yes. So do you send another email trying to better explain your point of view or request? You may get another response, only with more confusion or irritation. So you try another time to clarify, assuming that you are not now also frustrated and angry? The response that comes back could be even worse. So stop the madness.

When I was managing a team of managers, I had a Rule of Three: If you cannot resolve the issue in three emails, get on the phone or go visit the colleague in person. You can resolve communication issues much faster. Stop wasting time, energy, and emotions. We have found that this approach to communication is much more effective.

“Don’t let email dictate your priorities.”–Jeff Davidson, director of the Breathing Space Institute and author

Weekly Highlights Report

Weekly reports from your managers are a must, regardless of location. This is also true for Executive Committee members at a single location. At the end of each week, have each manager prepare a weekly highlight report and send it to an email alias that includes each team member. It should include the following:

- **Accomplishments:** Three to five bullet statements of what was accomplished during the week.
- **Next Week:** One to three statements of the next week's upcoming issues or challenges or where you might need a team member's help.
- **Other:** Anything pertinent, such as special guests or initiatives being rolled out in the upcoming week, to make everyone aware of the situation.

While it may seem like this is just another task to keep management happy, it is so much more than that. It actually requires each person to sit down and answer the question, "What did I accomplish this week?" While you may feel you were very busy for the week, what did you actually accomplish? It is a simple way to stop and acknowledge yourself, through the written word, regarding what you did.

Another benefit is that it helps keep the management team informed. You should not write out a large narrative. Rather, it needs to be a quick read for everyone. Many organizations require managers to submit a monthly report. This weekly activity helps jump-start that process, so that it is not tedious to compile information at the end of the month.

If you are consistent and timely with each of the weekly highlight reports, you will find them invaluable when it is your evaluation time. You will have a written journal of all your accomplishments and can simply pull out the most pertinent information. This becomes a time-saver for you and a win-win strategy. I learned this strategy from a former supervisor more than twenty years ago, and I still follow his sage advice.

"Weird and wonderful highlights of the week gone by."–Chris Evans, American actor

Criticism versus Feedback

I recently had a conversation with a former colleague, and she thanked me for helping her understand the difference between criticism and feedback. The word “criticism” is similar to the word “critique” in the artist’s world. She was accountable to a whole team of people in her new role. She thought it was her role to provide criticism and point out everything that was wrong. As you can imagine, it did not go over well. We had a great conversation about the difference between criticism and feedback. I explained that our role is to coach and provide to our team members feedback that is constructive, with an intention to help or improve a situation. Criticism is a judgment, and the intention is to find fault. What I also learned is that when we use certain words in the English language, they do not always translate well to managers from other countries. So we need to take the time to explain the intention and meaning of the word.

Focus on the intention. Ask yourself what it is you want to achieve. What is the intended outcome? Next, communicate with love. Connect your words to your feelings. Make sure there is love, not malice, in your heart.

Finally, we all can get better and improve. Yes, that includes managers and leaders. Think about the impact you want to make with this person in order to further develop them for the future. How you handle these types of situations can be your legacy.

Finally, after talking with the manager about how to provide feedback, role-play it, so they feel more confident.

So, how can you improve in providing feedback?

"Feedback is the breakfast of champions."–Ken Blanchard, American author and management expert

Mining Your Partners

Regardless of what industry you are in, if you are a leader or manager, you interact on occasion with a board of directors, industry advisory-committee members, or business partners. If you think about it, we are always asking each member to do something for our department or our company. They serve a role.

When was the last time you really got to know them? When was the last time you talked to them about their concerns in their business? When have you talked to them about what trends they are seeing in the business? When did you really begin to listen and understand what they are seeing in terms of trends in the industry or economy? Have you thought about how you might help them, rather than what you need from them? Have you asked them who they look up to in your industry? Who are their go-to people? Who are their mentors? Getting to know these people can help you contribute to them. Too many times in business, it becomes all about us instead about truly having a reciprocal win-win relationship. These relationships can be strengthened by this approach.

Another issue I have seen in some companies is "nepotism." The boards or advisory committees or groups of business partners are all made up of friends. The manager simply wants someone to rubber-stamp whatever they are proposing and agree with the manager's position. This can be problematic and lead to the demise of a company due to similar thinking rather than challenging the status quo. It is imperative that new thinking and new members are brought into the organization carefully.

I like to start with the people I know on the board or advisory committee and ask them for three referrals. I tell them we want to expand the membership, and we are looking for people they admire and people who represent a segment of the industry that is not represented at this time. I make phone calls, get to know them. I vet them with other colleagues.

Once I think we have found the right person to broaden our scope, they are invited for a tour, a lunch, and a discussion on how they might participate. They are informed of the responsibilities and time commitment. Once we gain commitment, we go from there.

You may have managers on your team who do not know how to expand and develop external relationships. Teach them how to find the best people to participate with you and improve your overall operation. You are mining for gold: the gold of their wisdom and expertise and fresh thinking. Explain why. It takes some effort, but the rewards are worth it.

"If your actions inspire others to dream more, learn more, and become more, you are a leader."–John Quincy Adams, 6th US President

B.A.N.K. ™ Personality Types

Have you ever gone into your supervisor's office with an idea for an initiative, and the response was a no instead of a yes? They flat-out did not buy your creative idea. You could not influence them. Well, you probably did not present the information in the way your supervisor could hear you. Every person is different. Their "communication and decision-making behavior" is unique. Every individual has a particular personality!

There are many excellent personality assessments in the marketplace today. One I have used is called the B.A.N.K. ™ Methodology. As many personality assessments on the market, it divides people into four personality/communication styles.

For B.A.N.K. ™, the four personalities are: Blueprint, Action, Nurturing, and Knowledge. I will explain each so you can be more effective in your presentation and communication style.

Not sure of your personality and what makes you tick or drives your buying behavior? You might be surprised! For fun, copy and paste www.mybankcode.com into your browser and find out. In less than 90 seconds, crack your code and get your free personalized assessment report. Share the link with your team and your manager rather than guessing about their personality codes.

The Blueprint Personality Boss

If your employee tends to be traditional, conservative, a planner, budget conscious, and risk averse, then your employee may be a Blueprint personality type.

So what is the best way to communicate with this personality type?

1. When you are presenting your idea, describe the amount of savings or impact the program could create for the department or organization.
2. Submit a plan with a specific goal, and list the sequential action steps to resolving the problem. It makes a stronger case if you can tie it back to the mission of the organization. Have a plan B for contingencies.
3. Make sure you address the time it will take and the costs involved.
4. Demonstrate you have performed due diligence. If possible, provide references or proof.
5. Define the benefit. Be consistent with your tone and intention.
6. Be prepared to manage or lead the project or the idea you are submitting. Blueprint personalities like it when you take the accountability for the project, meet the timeline, and stay within the approved budget.

The goal is to present a system or process for success. Give your employee time to process the information. Ask when you can schedule a follow-up. Confirm, “Does that work for you?” Do not pressure them for an immediate yes.

"Integrity: A name is the blueprint of the thing we call character. You ask what's in a name. I answer, it is just about everything you do." –Morris Mandel, American Jewish educator and journalist

The Action Personality Boss

If your employee tends to be high-energy, spontaneous, competitive, and driven, and if they enjoy lots of ideas, excitement, and attention, then your employee probably possesses entrepreneurial traits. According to B.A.N.K. ™ personality assessment, this is the Action personality type.

So how can I help you communicate with an Action personality?

1. Match their excitement when you present!
2. Offer the solution; remember, winning is important to them. In your presentation, use no more than three bullet statements.
3. Make it about them and how this can enhance their image, results, or revenue.

The goal is to present an idea that captivates their attention. After you give your idea, ask what they would like to do *now*.

"We are defined by our actions toward others, not others' actions toward us."–Anonymous

The Nurturing Personality Boss

Does your employee say, "Good morning" and check in with you? Ask how your weekend was or how your family is doing? If your employee tends to be relationship oriented, intuitive, and focused on authenticity, team work, and contribution, they may be a Nurturing personality type.

So how do you communicate with a Nurturing personality?

1. Get to know your employee on a personal level. Create a healthy relationship. Inquire about their family, animals, weekend, or hobbies.
2. Show your employee you truly care. Be authentic.
3. Appreciate the contribution the employee wants to make at work, in the family, and in the community. Realize that Nurturing personalities value harmony. Use an encouraging, hopeful tone in your statements.
4. Look them in the eye. Smile. Listen. Be fully present. Do not try to multitask.
5. Share your idea with details, and connect emotionally. Tie the idea back to the company's values or purpose.
6. Explain how your idea can help the company and the community.
7. After the implementation of the initiative, explain how the team could celebrate the success as a group to bond intensely!

The goal is to present an idea that makes an emotional connection and significant difference. After you present your idea, ask, "How do you feel about this?"

"Personality has the power to uplift, the power to depress, power to curse, and power to bless."–Paul Harris, entertainer

The Knowledge Personality Boss

You may have an employee who is a subject-matter expert, highly intelligent, extremely logical, appreciates technology, expects expertise and accuracy, and needs research and development to proceed. According to the B.A.N.K. ™ personality assessment at BANKCODE.com, this may indicate a Knowledge personality type.

So how do you communicate with your employee?

1. Start by answering the question, "What problem are you trying to solve?"
2. Present your idea in a logical manner. Stay with one problem at a time and one solution. If you are not the expert, bring an expert with you to co-present.
3. Use a smooth tone of voice without excitement or hyperactivity.
4. Build in charts, graphs, and assessments to validate your points.
5. Provide data, statistics, and facts. Make sure there are no errors or typos.
6. Provide all the options without the fluff.
7. Discuss the strategy.
8. End the presentation by leaving behind research report(s), a white paper, or a case study that supports your idea or presentation.
9. Do not expect an immediate decision.

The goal is to present an idea that makes logical sense and solves a problem. This supervisor needs time to analyze, process, and make the best decision. You will be disappointed if you want an immediate yes. After you present your idea, ask, "What do you think?"

You cannot influence a Knowledge personality. They are thorough thinkers and decide for themselves. Provide the right material, information, and time for them to do that. If they buy into your idea, they will be your hardcore supporters.

I have found that being present with the person with whom I am communicating and being sensitive to their style is much more effective than presenting from my personality or communication style. It is an investment of effort, but totally worth the reward.

"Knowledge will give you power but character respect."—Bruce Lee, Hong-Kong American actor, philosopher, and filmmaker

Creativity

Mind Mapping 101

Have you ever said yes to hosting a meeting, giving a speech, developing a training session, or facilitating at a conference, then right after that, had a feeling of dread? The thoughts go something like, *Why did I say yes?* Then for the next week or so, your mind is consumed with thoughts and worry about it.

I used to be this way until I discovered Mind Mapping. The concept was introduced to me by Tony Buzan, English author and educational consultant.

It is a technique that engages the whole brain. The applications and uses are endless. I usually start with a poster board and colored marking pens. I spend two minutes mapping out all the components for a presentation I need to create. I then put it away. In two minutes, I can get all my thoughts down about what I want to do for the presentation. My mind map is *my* mind map. It is as unique to me as your mind map will be to you. By putting your thoughts down on poster board, your thoughts are captured. The result is cleared-up space in your head, which reduces stress and allows for more creativity. I have taught this technique in a variety of settings. Before I can ask my employees or students to use it, I must teach them how to do so.

Mind mapping can be used in classes for students to take notes, highlight important issues, and study their notes in a text.

Teachers can use the technique to teach various things. Teachers can show students how to mind map to retain information longer. I use it when I want to create a new training program. Once I have my thoughts on the poster board, I then move to a Word document, a checklist, PowerPoint, or whatever I need to make sure I have everything by the time of the presentation.

This technique saves me time, reduces stress, and gives me a new level of creativity. If sitting with a poster board and markers is not your thing, there are software programs you can use instead. I like the software called Inspiration. I used Inspiration to create a visual of all the ways I currently use Mind Mapping. I also like the fact that Inspiration has a great set of templates for teachers when teaching specific concepts. Check it out!

Research this technique, and you will be amazed at how creative you become.

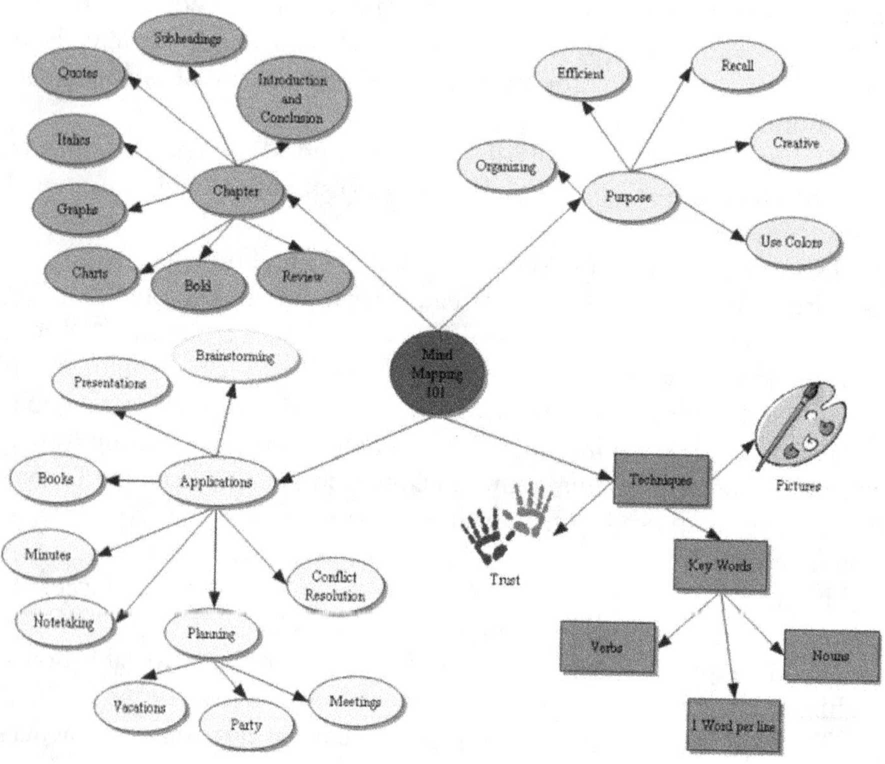

"Tell me, and I forget. Teach me, and I remember. Involve me, and I learn."–Benjamin Franklin, American author, printer, inventor, and diplomat

Brain Dump

Have you ever been so stressed out that you feel cannot add one more thought or idea in your brain, or else it will explode? Do you find yourself getting up in the middle of the night to make notes on your phone or paper? Do you find you cannot sleep or settle down because your mind is always racing? And yet, you feel like you are being less productive instead of more? I used to be that way, until I discovered a technique called a brain dump. It is painless!

For the first step, set aside an hour or two and get in front of your computer. You can use a document or spreadsheet application. Just start listing everything you have to do. List everything you have written down on a tablet, Post-It notes, calendar notes, lists from your inbox, and loose pieces of paper. List anything on your mind until you think you have exhausted all thoughts. Do not prioritize the list at this point. List professional things to do. List personal things to do. Look at your calendar. You might have two hundred to four hundred items listed, and that's fine. Save the document.

At this point, walk away from it. You have now have given your brain permission to have a blank slate. You also told your brain that all those things to do are now in a safe place. You begin to relax. You begin to have a space to create and be creative.

Get in the habit at the end of the day of deleting the items you have accomplished and adding new items that need to be created. Try this for thirty days, and see what happens.

This is a powerful tool and is better than a paper to-do list. With a paper to-do list, you are rewriting the list every day and wasting time. It is so easy to delete a line or add a line when it is in an electronic format.

Also, if you have a calendar system, use it for everything. Do not have a calendar for home and one for work. Have one calendar system. If you do not do this, something will get missed or double-booked. I see it all the time. If you are concerned about personal things being listed on your professional calendar system, just mark them as private.

I use this system and it works. If you get out of the habit for a few days, here is what you will notice. You are starting to get stressed again.

Thoughts are flying around in your head. Think to yourself, *When was the last time I actually updated my list?* My bet is that it has been a few days. Just get back in the habit and relax.

I do not use a color-code system. I do not prioritize these. I keep it simple so it will work. Do what will work for you.

Months later, I did create two additional columns: one for projects and another for calls. I used the project column to make sure the projects I need to complete are always present and serve as a visual reminder with a due date. I use the calls column to list all the calls I need to return, with phone numbers. When I find a few minutes between meetings, I make those calls, so they're completed within twenty-four hours of getting the message.

I cannot tell you what a difference this has made for me, and I hope it makes a difference for you.

"Clutter isn't just in your home, attic, garage, or office. Clutter is also in your mind, and distracts you from the amazing things you are meant to do."–Katrina Mayer, speaker, workshop leader, and author

Looping the Writing Process

If you have an upcoming speech or paper, and you need to prepare but have no idea where to start, looping might be the right process for you. Try this technique to help you generate new ideas or a new direction. When you don't think you have anything to say, or have too many thoughts in your head, or you are just stuck, try this three-part exercise:

First part

Start with a general topic and use it as the title of the paper. Write for at least fifteen minutes to see what you already know about the topic. Do not overthink it. Do not correct your work. Do not organize–just write your first thoughts on the topic. Do not censor your thoughts. Keep the pen on the paper moving through the whole process. Even if you are thinking, "I have nothing to say," write that down. The point is to keep the pen on the paper moving so you engage your brain. At the end of fifteen minutes, read over what you wrote. Circle the one word or few words that stand out to you.

Second part

Take the key word or words from the first exercise and that becomes your title for the second writing exercise. Write for at least fifteen minutes to see what you already know about the topic. Do not overthink it. Do not correct your work. Do not organize–just write out your first thoughts on the topic. At the end of fifteen minutes, read over what you wrote. Circle the one word or few words that stand out to you.

Third part

Take the key word or words from the second exercise, and that becomes your title for the third writing exercise. Write for at least fifteen minutes to see what you already know about the topic. Do not overthink it. Do not correct your work. Do not organize–just write first thoughts on the topic. At the end of fifteen minutes, read over what you wrote. Circle the one word or few words that stand out to you.

At this point, you are now focused on what you will write about or present. Your thinking is clearer. Think of this exercise as a funnel. You start out with a lot of ideas in your head, which is part one of the exercise. Then as you go through parts two and three, you are streamlining or focusing your thoughts. Now you know the direction to take. Happy looping!

"Start writing no matter what. The water does not flow until the faucet is turned on."–Louis L'Amour, novelist and short story writer

Inspiration Can Come from Anywhere

If you are a leader or a manager, much of your job is leading through inspiration. Where do you find your inspiration? I look at a variety of resources to keep me inspired. It might be a quotation of the day, for example. Other resources might include quotations, videos, speakers, podcasts, billboards, and books. Researching motivational videos on YouTube can be helpful to you and your team for themed meetings. *Ted Talks* are at the top of my list for learning about real issues in new ways. Podcasts and audiobooks are helpful to help you stay current and motivated as you commute to work. Researching quotations on the internet based on a theme, such as *Brainy Quotes,* is helpful, and you can use them in your communication. Having a book club that your organization participates in through printed books, e-books, or other source materials is a great way to focus everyone on a theme.

Some of my favorite books:

- *Start with Why: How Great Leaders Inspire Everyone to Action* by Simon O. Sinek
- *Leaders Eat Last* by Simon O. Sinek
- *The Tipping Point* by Malcolm Gladwell
- *Outliers* by Malcolm Gladwell
- *Blink* by Malcolm Gladwell
- *What the Dog Saw* by Malcolm Gladwell
- *The Dream Manager* by Matthew Kelly
- *The Energy Bus and Soup: A Recipe to Nourish Your Team and Culture* by Jon Gordon
- *The Carpenter: A Story about the Greatest Success Strategies* by Jon Gordon
- *Seed: Finding Purpose and Happiness in Life and Work* by Jon Gordon
- *Monday Morning Leadership* by David Cottrell

- *Monday Morning Mentoring* by David Cottrell
- *Tuesday Morning Coaching* by David Cottrell
- *Bringing out the Best in Others* by Thomas K. Connellan
- *Mindset* by Carol Dweck

You might have noticed a theme. I tend to like parable books that tell a story. With these, employees can visualize, relate to, and be emotionally connected to the content. I like to read, research, and be inspired. I like to inspire.

What are your favorites?

"Don't count the days. Make the days count."–Muhammad Ali, heavyweight champion boxer

Marketing

Does Your Building Tell a Story?

If no one were available to walk guests and visitors around your building, and they toured the building on their own, what would your building say? Think of your building like an art gallery. Is there a logical flow? It should be interesting. Is there easy-to-read directional signage? Are the exhibits, kiosks, or plasma screens all labeled, and do they tell a story about the company operation? Where are the gaps? What can be improved?

This is just the beginning. If your operation is a university, community college, vocational, or technical school, here are departmental suggestions for next steps.

Admissions Sales

If you have an internal admissions sales team, what are they saying when leading prospective students on tours? Yes, the college has a script, but what is each person really saying? As a new president at each school I led, I met with the Admissions director and explained that I wanted to have each Admissions representative take me on a tour. The goal was to add value to me personally and to the operation. I requested we partner together on this. My directors of Admissions were always great and agreed. This was true even for the remote locations and the directors at those locations.

I would set up an appointment with each Admissions sales representative and have them take me on tour. While it initially caused anxiety, they soon learned I wanted to learn from them. I wanted to know what they thought was important and should be highlighted. I got to know them in a totally different way. I asked questions about programs, resources, support services, scholarships, career services, the library, clubs, etc. Each person added to my knowledge base. After the tour, I recorded special things I learned from each person.

Academics

Next, I asked each department director to give me a tour and explain their program, area, equipment, and resources as well as concerns. I asked them questions related to Admissions on what they wanted highlighted. Not surprisingly, the department directors and faculty encouraged the Admissions representatives to stop by with prospective students and talk. They wanted to be asked questions about the field, jobs, classes, and equipment during their office hours. They wanted a true partnership. I then recorded what they said.

Support Services

The next step was visiting with each manager accountable for support services. I asked them to teach me about their department. I was in the role of student, and they were the teachers. I learned so much.

Finally, I took all my notes and worked with the director of Admissions. We created a written tour guide. We outlined the order of the tour, highlighted each department and service and specialty areas within the building. We then held a joint meeting. I thanked everyone for their generous contribution to me and the organization.

Then the director of Admissions took over and trained the team. The team first reviewed the document. Then the director took the entire team on a tour. They learned new information and expectations for going forward. The consistency was incredible and gave us a great new tool for training new hires. The directors at the remote locations did the same thing after I visited the locations. I can assure you the personal benefit to me was incredible. After many, many tours, I felt like I knew the building inside and out.

So, how can you use this idea in your operation?

"Those who tell stories rule society."–Plato, Greek philosopher

A Regional Marketing Approach When You Are Not Totally in Charge

As a leader, have you ever been a part of an organization that had multiple departments–such as sales, community outreach, public relations, marketing and advertising, and social media–accountable for marketing? Perhaps you had direct control over some areas but not others. Maybe some areas on the organizational chart illustrate your dotted-line relationship or accountability? Ever felt like these departments were working in silos? Ever felt like there are gaps or duplications of work? Did you just read the various reports and just accept the situation as the status quo, or did you apply innovative thinking?

I found a strategy that I think works. It is critical to have the key players get together once a quarter in order to build the success of the company. The ideal situation would be face-to-face, but in reality this may not be possible; however, technology can assist. For the initial meeting, share the vision of what you want to accomplish with each department head. Seek permission from the department head for a member of their unit to attend, accountable for marketing. You need to build buy-in, because when you take them out of productivity even for a half-day meeting, there has to be a return on the investment.

- Prepare to have a successful meeting.
- Plan out the details: the room, the time, the date, the technology, the food, water, pens, agenda, handouts, technology requirements, supplies, the air temperature, etc.
- Decide on the theme of the meeting.
- Build in inspiration with a video to support the theme.
- Build in time for introductions by name, position title, territory, and brief discussion of their role.
- Create an agenda with a purpose and anticipated outcomes.
- Send out the agenda in advance.

- Have each company participant share their top ten clients, goals or metrics, territory, and products, and bring sample marketing collateral materials.
- Review the metrics and the data. Opinions do not support growth today. We are operating in a data-driven world. Analyze the data. This is where robust conversations can occur.
- Caution: If the first meeting does not provide value, it is unlikely the participants will return next quarter. This takes effort, and is totally worth it. The meeting needs to be valuable the first time out!
- Once you have built trust within the team, ask each participant to share one of the challenges in their role. Ask how this group can help support their efforts and challenges. Strong partnerships are formed this way.
- Set the date for the next meeting before you adjourn to make sure you know who will attend the next time. Take minutes and distribute them within forty-eight hours to seventy-two hours.
- As time goes on, the team will be able to determine gaps and overlaps and suggest new ideas for solving these challenges.

Change happens every day. Company changes include layoffs, restructures, terminations, new territories, new products, and new hires. If one of your participants leaves the company or role, and a replacement is added, the new colleague will need to be personally invited to the next marketing meeting. You will need to explain the value and importance of the meeting. Explain how getting to know everyone can actually help them be more successful and expedite their success. Provide samples of past meeting minutes so they can get caught up. Wishing you the most productive marketing meetings and improved results!

"Marketing without data is like driving with your eyes closed."
–Dan Zarrella, social media scientist

Meeting Management

Are You Running an Effective Meeting? What Would Your Employees Say?

Have you ever stopped to calculate the cost of holding a meeting? The time it takes? The salaries of the people in attendance? When you start to think about it that way, you may want to reinvent the way you hold meetings. The point is, don't hold a meeting just to hold a meeting.

The role of the leader is to set the tone for the meeting. In most cases, this will be a positive tone. Whether these meetings are group meetings or one-on-one meetings, the day and time should be set. An agenda should be created in advance of the meeting and sent to all participants. It also helps to ask for agenda items to be included from participants. You may have a standing agenda template with standard issues to be discussed to keep you on point.

Decide on the purpose of the meeting. Is this meeting informational, brainstorming, problem-solving, strategic planning, operational review, etc.? Decide on who should attend. Just because you are holding a meeting does not mean the same people should attend each time. It will depend on the topics of the agenda. This will actually save you time and money if you have the right people attending the meeting and they are not an afterthought.

Meetings should start and end on time. This is a respect issue for all involved. I find that opening with a positive story about the organization or an employee works well. It could be a quick two- to five-minute inspirational video on a topic. It could be a quotation that sets the tone of the meeting. It could be the metrics achieved. It could be something as simple as sharing something positive personally or within the department.

It sets the expectation. Too many times, we as managers just focus on problems. Obviously, solving problems is the reason we are paid.

As the leader, your job is also to inspire and motivate your team. The meeting is the perfect place to do this. Your employees should leave that meeting feeling better than when they walked in, more focused and clearer about what needs to be done by whom and by when.

During the meeting, each action item should have a person assigned accountability and a timeline. The date should be set for the next meeting before leaving the current meeting. This will provide clarity. The date of the next meeting is important even if it is a standing meeting, because of employee travel schedules, vacation, and possible other commitments. The leader needs to know who to expect at the next meeting or if others should attend or if the meeting should be delayed.

Finally, minutes should be taken and sent out within twenty-four to seventy-two hours. The minutes will be fresh enough in the participants' minds and a reminder of what is expected for the next meeting. Once you set the tone and expectation, your team will respect how important the meeting is, how they can contribute, and what their accountability is. If you model it, they will follow.

What strategies do you use that are effective and inspiring?

"Management is doing things right; leadership is doing the right things."—Peter F. Drucker, American business consultant

Slaying the Silos

Are you managing a group of individual departments? Does it seem like each department does an effective job in a silo, and yet it does not feel right? Does it seem like the right hand does not know what the left hand is doing? Do the company culture and values seem misaligned with reality? Does it seem like the mission and values are written but not modeled?

What I have found is that it is up to the leader to bring groups of people together to change the situation. Provide opportunities to train together as a group or across departments, or come together for problem-solving or brainstorming scenarios to solve real operational problems. Think about departments that have to work together but do not necessarily have opportunities to meet.

Here are a few examples from my university days. After you have spent the first thirty days listening, meeting, and getting connected to your new employees, you will find golden nuggets in their words.

Enrollment Team Meeting attendees: Receptionist, Admissions advisors, Admissions support staff, Student Support Services advisors, testing coordinator, admittance essay review team, registrar, Financial Aid advisors, New Student Orientation staff member, housing coordinator. List all the people who participate in your particular process. Ours included roles from the initial contact through acceptance and new-student orientation. Each person is integral to success and timely matriculation process.

Example:

- Diagram the complete enrollment process.
- Hold a meeting and visually demonstrate the role of each person in the process to show the ideal way for it to go. Point out any lags causing a delay due to process or people.
- Share the enrollment timeline expectations.
- Provide a handout that lists the sequential steps to the enrollment process.

- Set up groups of people from mixed departments. Have them brainstorm solutions to aid in the enrollment process to reduce time, errors, or paperwork. Record the responses.
- Send out minutes and begin to operationalize.
- Hold a second meeting shortly after, but before this, solicit feedback from each manager on specific problems they are having that need a resolution. Develop mini case studies from what they share.
- Hold your next meeting with the same group, and seek input on the case-study examples. Take minutes and operationalize. Train to your new expectations and processes. You may find some real savings in terms of time, resources, and frustrations.

Think through areas within your organization where there is no formal structure to meet but a need to develop relationships to improve the overall operation and reduce the silos. In my example, groups that typically do not meet are:

- First-year faculty members with first-year academic advisors
- First-year faculty members with first-year academic advisors, student tutors, librarian, and the Academic Success Center staff
- Admissions, student coaches, Financial Aid advisors, registrar, and Career Services
- Student-support service, the Academic Success Center faculty, and student tutors
- Academics, Admissions, and Career Services
- Career services, internship coordinator, professional-development/career development faculty members, and alumni staff members.

Over time, you will discover the magic in bringing people together! Go out and be the silo slayer!

"Silo walls between business units that impede cooperation and communication need to come down."–Howard Stringer, British businessman

Operations

Mission-Focused Decision-Making 101

Most organizations today have a mission statement. For some organizations, the mission is central to everything they do. It helps the team members define what and how they do what they do. The mission is part of their vision, values, and culture. It is a unifying theme. It is imbedded throughout the organization. It is a way of being or a set of behaviors.

Some organizations, however, have a mission statement but give only lip service to the statement. You can also hear most employees say, "Yes, that's what it says, but that is not what we do." It might be stated on the company website or printed and framed throughout the building, but that is all it is. When you walk into a company or business, you have a feeling about the organization. You can almost tell whether or not it is well-run. It is a feeling, whether you are aware of this or not.

For me, the mission statement is the frame. It helps keep me grounded. As a leader, you will be presented with a lot of ideas by employees. You will be presented with budget requests, time requests, or new project initiatives, to name a few examples.

When I was a new leader, I often found it hard to decide whether to approve or deny an initiative or request. Everyone wants to hear that their idea, project, or request has been approved. What I have learned over my years of experience is that deciding this has become easy. I simply refer back to our mission statement. If the request will forward and support our mission, then it will be a yes–and I approve the concept. Obviously, plans, details, and budgets have to be worked through. If the project does not support our mission, I do not approve the request. It might be a good idea, but if it is not in keeping with our mission, I cannot support it. This exercise keeps me grounded. I also teach my managers that for a request to be considered, it must be in keeping with our mission. Your mission is central to everything you do.

Good luck in every endeavor you take on and forwarding your mission!

"Mission is about people, not projects."–Dr. Todd Engstrom, executive pastor of ministry strategies

Director of First Impressions

I am often interested in how management makes certain decisions about staffing, salary, and priorities. In this world of high technology and high touch, a company has to make the decision whether or not to have a human being answer the phone or staff the front desk of an office. Many companies opt for an automated system. I am sure there are good reasons why the companies decided to go that route, but let's not think about it from the company perspective. Let's think about it from the customer perspective. How many times have you called a company and had an automated service answer the call? How long did you have to wait? How many times were you transferred? How many times did you input a number to get the department you thought you needed, only to find it was not correct and had to start all over? How did you feel? Frustrated?

I once worked for a college where we had a receptionist, Elizabeth, answer the phones and handle incoming visitors. She left our company, and we had an opportunity to hire a new employee. Elizabeth had set a whole new standard for customer service. With each phone call, you could hear the smile in her voice. Each visitor inquiry or student's question, she handled with ease and grace. No matter how busy she was, you never heard stress in her voice. She truly cared and was very special. I had never experienced anything like it, and I have worked with some amazing people. We all felt proud to work at the college because of Elizabeth. She set the tone for every inquiry or interaction.

Our Human Resources director had a conversation with her and asked her, if she could change her title, what it would be. She said, "I want to be called the 'Director of First Impressions.'" Truthfully, she was right. We changed her title, updated her name tag, and gave her a substantial increase in pay. She did not ask for anything, but she deserved everything.

This example was a pivotal moment in my career. It really had me rethink where we spend our money and how important the first impression is. This position is not a minimum-wage position. How much money would you spend to make a great first impression? How much have you spent on marketing and advertising, but when it comes to staffing, you cut corners?

Elizabeth taught us many great lessons, and for that I will be forever grateful. Do you have an Elizabeth?

"You will never have a second chance to make a good first impression."–Liketoquote.com

Deer in the Headlights

Have you ever seen a person walking through your building, and they have the "deer in the headlights" look? More importantly, have you seen staff walk by this person and not acknowledge them in any way?

Have you ever noticed people in a restaurant, and they have the same look, but no one seems to notice? I am a people-watcher, and I never cease to be amazed about waiters, busboys, and service personnel who walk by a customer who clearly needs something and nevertheless is ignored.

Clearly, both of these situations are training opportunities and require immediate action. If you do not set the expectation as the manager, nothing will change.

What do you want? State what you want in the team meeting. The training goes something like this: "You all have noticed that there are multiple entrances into our building, and sometimes they can be confusing. How many of you have noticed in our building people who looked uncertain as to where to go?" Most probably, the majority of your team will raise their hands. "So when you notice this, what should you do?" You will get a variety of answers. Once the employees participate, I recommend you state the expectation. For me, it goes like this:

"We want our visitors to feel welcome when they enter our building. I know the layout of the building can be confusing, even though we have signage. My request is that when you are walking down the hall, pay attention, and when you see someone who is uncertain, ask them how you can help or who they are going to see.

"Once they tell you who they are going to see, walk them to the front desk, and have the front-desk staff member check them in. Have the receptionist announce the visitor to the person or department. Then you walk the visitor to the person or department. Do not simply give directions. Take an extra few minutes and extend hospitality to show the visitor the way. It is a small gesture, but means a great deal to our visitors. As the manager, model it for your employees. This is not a case of 'tell and not show.' It is a case of 'show and tell and show.'"

"Helping a person will not necessarily change the world, but it will change the world for that person."–thatonerule.com

People Will Often Surprise You

More than thirty years ago, I was managing a luxury hotel. It was such an honor to work at a beautiful property and with great people. It was also stressful. Little did I know, the hotel was having cash-flow problems. I had been in similar situations before but not quite as desperate.

I have always been a manager who shared the good and the bad with my employees to keep them informed about how we were doing. I communicated each month through a thirty-minute, all-employee meeting. I had worked at the hotel before in a different management position and still knew many of the staff, which helped. They knew when I said something, it was the truth. We had a multitude of problems and worked through each one. It was stressful because I was not sure we would make payroll every other week. I knew if I had a bit of time, we could turn the situation around, and I could not let the stress of the situation show.

It seemed to me every day one of our housekeepers, Janet, would find me in the hotel and complain. She could not understand how we could work in such a beautiful hotel and run short of supplies. On another day, the complaint was the hourly rate they were making or when they were going to get a raise. Each day consisted of a new complaint. I listened. I liked her and her spunk. No matter the complaint, she always had a smile on her face. I truly understood how she felt. At the time, I felt nothing could be done in the moment, and that is not how I like to operate. She really got to me.

Finally, one day I invited Janet to my office. I talked to Janet for a while and learned about her background and experience. I learned she had a high-school education, she really liked working at the hotel, and she was smart. She pointed out a lot of problems. I asked her if she wanted to be the "General Manager for the Day." This was long before job-sharing or cross-departmental training was the norm. She jumped at the chance. She was going to change everything in a day.

I smiled. I told her she needed to learn about our financials and budgeting. She was a great student. We spent the day together, and she took it all in. I am truly not sure what happened that day, but there was a personal transformation.

The next day when I went downstairs to the housekeeping department to greet the housekeepers good morning before they went to clean the rooms, I saw Janet—or rather, I should say I heard Janet. She was a woman on a mission. She told each housekeeper to prevent waste, to save money, and to share their great ideas. From that day forward, Janet became my budget advocate and partner in turning our hotel around, and for that I will be eternally thankful. Listen to each person. Never underestimate the talent you surround yourself with—they are our future.

"Once in a blue moon, people will surprise you . . . and once in a while, people may even take your breath away."—*Grey's Anatomy*, American television medical drama

Doing More with Less

Have you ever been short on resources? If yours is like most organizations, each year you are asked to do more with less. As the manager, how do you continue to improve the operation, keep morale high, and do more with less? How do you keep employees engaged?

Each year, there is a report that lists the top five to ten reasons employees stay in a job. What surprises many new managers is that salary is never listed in the top five reasons. Usually, the first reason is that the employee likes or respects the person for whom they work. Employees do not quit organizations; they quit people. Employees stay if they believe in the mission of the organization, if they can contribute, feel respected, are trained, and so on. So, what do you do to keep people connected and engaged?

It is all in the details. You need to show people in small ways that you care. Some of these things will be based on the individual. Sometimes, you will plan group activities. Most of the time, you do not have a budget for such things, so what do you do?

Did you know you can research creative ways to bring teams together? Did you know there is a national day for almost everything? Or a national week for something? So, depending on your organization, look to see what "national days of" support your mission. What days or weeks support your vision or values? Look to see if there are days or weeks that are community-based that support the overall well-being of the community. Plan certain days throughout the year and theme the event based on this. It can be a potluck or a morning coffee break or an afternoon ice-cream break planned to bring people together for a short period of time in a new way.

Have fun connecting in a whole new way!

"Doing more with less is a crucial principle to learn; especially if you are going to be in business in a rapidly changing world."—Robert Kiyosaki, American finance author, investor

Networking–The Connector

I used to dread networking events, but then I changed my mindset. When I was a new manager, I tended to stay to myself and wait for the obligatory event to be over. I sort of missed the point of the networking event. Over time, I realized I could learn a lot if I changed my outlook.

So the first change I made was to invite a more outgoing colleague to go with me. They loved these types of events and liked being asked to go along. He or she was great in introducing me to some of their friends, colleagues, or new contacts. This helped me learn a lot and begin to feel more comfortable at networking events. They were so genuine in their approach. They focused on quality conversations. Now I can do this on my own, but I had to learn how from my outgoing friends.

What now works for me is to have a purpose when I attend a networking event. I concentrate on meeting one or two new people. I bring my business cards along. My purpose is to concentrate on the new people. I focus on having a quality conversation. I want to begin to know them and what interests them.

I listen for how I can help them or connect them with someone I know. They may have an open position at their company. They may be looking for a technology solution. They might be looking for someone in my industry with whom I can put them in contact. They may just need someone to listen to their frustrations and let them vent. These networking events are not about me. They are about the one or two people I meet.

Have you ever seen someone at a networking event as they speed through the room, shake hands, and quickly go on to the next person? There is no eye contact. They act like serial networkers. They barely remember your name. How does that make you feel?

On the other hand, how do you feel when someone asks you questions about yourself? Remembers your name? Looks you in the eyes? I think you probably feel great. So think about these tips the next time you are invited to a networking event. With a little preparation, you might create a contact or friend forever. Happy networking!

"The currency of real networking is not greed but generosity."
–Keith Ferrazzi, global thought leader, author, and speaker

Postmortems

Have you ever worked for a company for several years and noticed how much things change with personnel, ideas, and practices? Have you ever noticed there were some good ideas or initiatives five or six years ago that no longer exist? Do you ever wonder how that happens? Did the person who led the change leave the organization? Good ideas should not start and stop with one person.

From my experience, if you want your organization to grow stronger, you have to document the procedure, event, or initiative. The greater the detail, the better. Document why you are doing what you are doing. I agree with the author Simon Sinek in his book titled *Start With Why,* but I believe it goes beyond just your mission. It should be threaded throughout every activity to make sure it is still part of your company mission of why you do what you do. Then document the agenda items. The documentation should include who does what, where, how, by when, and what resources are needed.

Once the event or initiative takes place, hold a postmortem. Most organizations are great at holding planning meetings; however, many lack the consistent strategy of holding postmortems after each event. The idea is to review what went well and what needs to be changed. Then document so the next time you hold the event, it is even better. Go through the exercise every time. This habit forces the managers and the leaders to use new "muscles" to improve the overall operation and build continuous improvement. You will be amazed at what you can accomplish. This helps introduce team members quickly into the process and culture.

"Openness, transparency, and candor: these three characteristics are required."—Warren Bennis, Daniel Goleman, and James O'Toole,in *How Leaders Create a Culture of Candor*

Spring Cleaning; or Company is Coming

At least once or twice a year, we would schedule "spring cleaning" at our organization and additional sites. Truthfully, we did this sometimes to prepare for VIP guests. Sometimes, we did this to make sure we were in compliance with current-year resources such as marketing materials, brochures, regulations, and published statistics. Sometimes we needed to discard dated materials. Whatever the reason we had for scheduling spring cleaning, it was amazing what happened.

The employees were notified of the day or days we scheduled this. You need a communication plan to do this effectively. We would bring in additional trash receptacles, recycling bins, and bins for confidential shredding. We would allow employees to wear jeans to work. We would provide a lunch or host a potluck to help bring everyone together on cleaning day.

Everyone was involved. We also included those pesky storage areas that seem to be the dumping ground for supplies that nobody wants or an open space employees think they can store something out of sight, out of mind. Each area would have a designated person held accountable to make sure it was clean. Sometimes we found supplies we did not know we had. Sometimes we found office supplies all over the building. We would then consolidate those supplies in specific departments or a new designated storage area.

At the end of the day, the managers would all walk through the building, going into each area. It was a whole new set of eyes to make sure the area was clean and marketing materials were properly displayed. We did not miss anything. The other purpose was to show off our newly cleaned areas.

It may sound a bit silly, but I can assure you the next day when everyone came to work, they felt better. Ridding areas of clutter allowed our employees to feel proud to work in our organization.

It is a lot like when you have company coming to your home. What do you do? You clean. You present your home in an inviting new way. You want your guests to feel welcome and good about being in your space. You want to be proud. Why not have the same thing at work? Happy spring cleaning.

"Spring cleaning is not just about sorting through things and getting rid of clutter. It's about taking stock of who you are and how others see you. It's a chance to redefine yourself, to change expectations, and to remember it is *never* too late to recapture who you were or to aim for who you want to be."–Anonymous

Top Ten Things You Need to Know

Whether it is new employees or new students, there is always key information each person needs to know. What is it in your organization? When you hold an orientation, how much of the information is retained? Not as much as you wish. Going back and revisiting the top ten policies or issues is always a good idea. In the follow-up, the groups will probably be a smaller audience. Each person will have time to reflect and ask questions. Repetition is a good thing.

If you do not know what the top ten items might be, ask your team. Think about areas where employees and students fail or come up against problems, and you will quickly generate your top-ten list.

I made it a practice to go into every new class each session and speak with the students for thirty to forty-five minutes. I gave each person a questionnaire with a list of the top ten most important items to understand at the university. Each person could work with a partner. This helped with building connections. Each pair was given ten minutes to search for the answers to list the top ten most important things to know at the university. The teams could search the portal, talk with the partner, or search through our website. This scavenger-hunt activity gave them practice on navigating through the university tools and learning about resources available to them. The hands-on activity reinforced what they had been told at orientation and might not have retained.

Then we conducted a review with the teams, providing the answers. We discussed each item. I know I wished someone had done this for me when I was in college or starting a new job. I probably would not have made some of the mistakes I made. Today, I would take this one step further and leave them with an infographic to hold on to for review when needed.

Examples could include:

- Satisfactory academic policy and how it affects the individual
- Security expectations/badges
- Fire drill

- Accreditation
- Scavenger hunt on your company portal
- Career Services
- Support Services
- APA format expectations
- Plagiarism
- Resources
- Key personnel contacts depending on the audience
- Posting on social media–LinkedIn vs Facebook expectations

You can provide an FAQ sheet. You can then have an open discussion and have them ask you questions. The final part of the session is to share your contact information with the group–email, office phone number, and/or cell phone. You can instruct employees in how to make an appointment to talk further. So, what are your top ten in your organization?

"I'm looking for the unexpected. I'm looking for things I have never seen before."–Robert Mapplethorpe, artist

Program Creep

Have you ever worked for an organization, been on a board, or served as a volunteer member of an association? If you have participated or been employed for a number of years in the same organization, you might have experienced this. The leadership changes each year, or every so often. With each new leader comes new ideas and a new direction. The new leaders are often passionate and want to do a good job. Each person brings more and more ideas and programs to the role.

Then one day, you find that all this good work might have gone too far. I call it "program creep." The people in the organization or association have the best intentions, but it has gotten out of hand. Upon further examination, you realize that your organization has now become an organization that wants to be all things to all people. When that happens, your organization becomes ineffective. You lose your way. Your organization has to stand for something, be known for something.

I believe that on an annual basis, leadership should conduct a complete review of the organization. Do the initiatives you have underway support the mission? Do they support the values or competencies of the organization? Or was it just a good idea someone had? This is a great time to use the Stop, Start, and Continue exercise. What should we stop doing? What should we start doing? What should we continue to do? This is a healthy exercise for any department to practice. Many organizations roll out new initiatives each year, year over year, piling more and more on their employees. At some point, it becomes too much. They literally cannot do their jobs but may feel they cannot say anything to stop the madness. Sometimes less is more. How would your organization stack up?

"Having too many ideas is not always a good thing."–Paul Arden, author

Secret Shopper, Sort Of

We all know to shop our organizations. This can look a lot of different ways, depending on the organization and what you want to learn. You certainly know to call during operating hours and see how you are greeted and transferred. You are listening for how quickly and competently the phone is answered. Does the person know how to transfer the call? Does the person transfer you to someone who can really help you? Were they listening?

When was the last time you called your operation after hours? What I mean by that: when was the last time you called every extension in your operation or had someone do it for you? Experience is great in a management position, but sometimes it gets in the way of looking at things in a fresh way. I recently went back through this exercise, calling every extension listed in our phone tree. I was listening for personal voice mails and what each employee was saying.

What did I learn? I found we had some great personal voice mails that really connected with our guests and colleagues. I also found some people had never set up their voice mails. I also found that in some instances, the directory listed one name and another person had that extension. I also found extensions listed for positions in which we had no one employed.

After conducting this exercise, I found that our IT department was very frustrated with the situation but did not feel they had the power to change it. After we discussed it, we held a meeting to share the results of the call campaign. The purpose was to help employees go back and create a personal voice-mail message that was in keeping with our mission. We also had our IT department staff members on standby to help those employees who were uncertain about how to set up voice mail. We gave the employees sample greetings to use. We explained the "why" for doing this. Technology is great–but only if we use it properly. It is the little things that can trip up an operation. When was the last time you conducted a similar campaign?

"There is always room in your life for thinking bigger, pushing limits, and imagining the impossible."–Tony Robbins, author, actor, professional speaker

Change Management

Every organization faces change if it wants to improve and remain current. Every manager is then charged with communicating those changes to the employees. What happens many times is that senior leadership has shared details about the change initiative with the managers. The managers are then expected to communicate the change. The manager dutifully feels the need to communicate immediately and has not really thought the changes through. In my experience, it does not go well.

Imagine you are the manager in charge of the communication. Think through what you are going to say before you say it. Describe the change as completely you can. Before you describe the change, tell your employees what is *not* changing, so they are listening. Then tell them what *is* changing. State how it will impact your employees, the department, or the organization. Each employee is listening from the perspective of how it will affect them personally. As you are talking, employees are thinking thoughts like these: *Do I still have a job; is my salary being reduced; are my hours changing?* These thoughts are uppermost in their minds.

If you do not know certain aspects of the change initiative, ask your leadership before you communicate the change. Ask yourself, what is your vision of the best possible outcome? And write it down, so you can share the vision. Your employees can imagine the same thing. People tend to be more visual, so anytime you can paint a picture, you are more likely to be able to fulfill the vision. Your employees need to be able to see it.

Think about what the strengths of your group/department are in undertaking this change. Now stop and think through the obstacles to the change. What will prevent you from reaching your goal? Many times, managers do not think through this critical step, and that can delay or derail the change initiative. Now list the action steps for your communication plan–who will resist, who needs to be involved, and who needs to buy in. Know there will initially be resistance. In the beginning, you will have ten percent to twenty percent who are totally with you and ready to make the change happen. The next group will need to process the information and then will become part of the plan.

Another percentage will be undecided—and some are never going to get on board. Ideally, those never accepting the change will be a small percentage of the total group. There is a cycle to how people feel when change happens. It is similar to the death-and-dying cycle of shock, denial, sadness or anger, grief, and then acceptance. Be empathetic to where your people are in the process. Their feelings are real.

Decide what your timetable is for making this change, from start to finish. What new skills, knowledge, and attitudes are needed to make this change? Think this through carefully, as there will be downtime, frustration, and lower productivity while employees are gaining new skills and knowledge. Plan for it. If you don't think this is true, think back to the last major software upgrade your company undertook and how long it took before the employee base became proficient again.

Finally, how will you acknowledge, recognize, and celebrate this change? Many managers just go on to the next task and do not stop and acknowledge the "win" for the team. This is a huge mistake. Over time, morale goes down if you continue to push without recognition. Likely, by following these steps, your change initiatives will improve over time. Good luck in implementing successful change!

“You have to change to succeed.”–J. T. Foxx, real-estate investor, speaker, philanthropist, and world’s #1 wealth coach

Survey Tools and Reports

I really believe that as a manager, your job is twofold: you are either teaching or learning, no matter in what industry you work. Whether it is a new manager who just started a job or it is you who just started a job, it is imperative you understand the tools, resources, and reports.

In every job I have taken on, I've noticed similar themes. One, there are more data and reports available than you have time to digest. Over time, I realized I needed to ask my supervisor what the most important reports were to him or her. Which reports should I concentrate on daily, weekly, or monthly?

If I were a new manager, I would ask my manager to go through the reports with me, so I had a clear understanding of the data and how it could be used. If I were the training manager, I would walk the new employee through the reports, so they had a clear understanding of the company standards and for what we were striving. Helping managers and employees understand the data is key. More and more decisions today are data driven, and if you do not understand the data, you are behind.

The next opportunity is to investigate the survey tools your company uses. It is very important that you understand what the company is measuring, the results for which they are looking, and how you can impact process improvement. I worked for a company many years ago that had a great survey instrument, but no one used it as intended. One of two things happened: one group totally misunderstood the data, and the other group ignored the report altogether. I found out that they did not understand the reports from the survey instrument or how to use the data for process improvement.

I went back to the vendor who sold us the instrument. I learned everything I could from them. I designed a training program around it that was practical and simple to understand. The results were amazing. The faculty bought in regarding the instrument and began using the resources. The department heads saw the value as a coaching tool. As a new manager on the team, I was not afraid to admit I did not understand how to properly interpret the data from this instrument.

Two years later, this company asked me to come and present how we used the data and reports as a best practice for others to emulate. One simple set of questions led to creating a system-wide best practice.

It is not a sign of weaknesses to admit you do not know something when you are first on the job. Ask questions, research, and learn. Take what you learn and help others. Where are the opportunities at your company?

"Accept yourself, your strengths, your weakness, and your truths; and know what tools you have to fulfill your purpose."–Steve Maraboli, speaker, bestselling author, and behavioral scientist

Layoffs and Terminations

In all the years I have held a leadership or management position, I have never known anyone to enjoy having to terminate or lay off an employee, even if justified. The causes for termination and layoffs vary. If it gets to the point of terminating an employee, a lot of work has gone into this decision. There has been documentation, coaching, and an effort to turn the situation around, if done properly. No matter how much effort has been invested, the manager and employee must have an equal desire and effort to turn the situation into a positive. Sadly, more times than not, the situation ends in termination. It is not easy for the employee to hear those words. It is not easy for the manager to deliver the message.

Layoffs seem to be more prevalent than ever before and occur across all industries. Usually the decision is made to reduce costs, change direction, redirect a product line, or replace personnel with technological improvements. Once again, the manager never wants to have to deliver this kind of message. Employees do not want to hear the layoff decision and how it will impact their lives.

I have seen organizations handle both layoffs and terminations poorly, and some humanely. My experience says that in the case of terminations, deliver the news quickly in a face-to-face setting. I walk the employee through the next steps. Do not argue with the employee. Listen and then help the employee absorb and process the situation. Treat them humanely. Do not parade them out of the building in a walk of shame. Depending on your company policy, allow them the opportunity to take their personal items, say goodbye, and leave the building. In some cases, it might be better for the person to return after hours to remove their personal items. In the case of layoffs, these employees did nothing wrong. Deliver the message, walk them through the next steps, and allow them to say goodbye to their friends and colleagues. Treat them with dignity and respect. What I find shocking is how some managers treat these employees with no regard. Remember that just a few minutes prior to delivering the news, they were considered good employees contributing to the overall mission of the organization. They are still good people. When managers do anything less than treat them humanely, things go poorly. Let the employees know how you will support them in their job pursuit. Let them know what company resources are available to them. Let them know about filing for unemployment. While this situation is never easy, the way you treat people in these situations is critical in the moment and for years going forward. The employees may not remember the exact words you used, but they will remember for the rest of their lives how they were treated. What memory do you want to create?

"Life never presents us with anything which may not be looked upon as a fresh starting point, no less than a termination."–Andre Gide, French novelist and essayist

Survey Apathy

Ever wonder why our clients or students get survey apathy? How many customer-service assessments do you send out? What do you do with the data? How does it help your organization? I have seen a lot of university survey apathy by students when they complete surveys throughout the school year. If there is a low response rate, you might be suffering from survey apathy.

In order to solve this, tell the participants how the data will be used. Once you have the results, circle back after reviewing with your team and give the students/clients the results.

Choose the top three items with which the students are pleased. Then give the students the top three things they are displeased with or think need improvement. Then tell the students what you are going to do about it. In some cases, your explanation might state that more time is needed and the Executive Committee will be reviewing it. In some cases, you will have an immediate response, whether positive or negative. Sometimes the response is a restatement of a policy that they did not understand. Sometimes their expectations are not the same as the institutions. You will know how to handle this.

Provide the feedback in the medium that works the best for your organization. We found that emails, paper, or announcements did not work. We chose to use our plasma screens around the campus to let students know every quarter how we were all doing. We called it: "We Asked; You Said." When they saw these headlines, they knew what was coming. This feedback loop let them know we valued their feedback, and our response rates went up dramatically over time. The other things it did was help the Executive Committee be fully informed of the issues from the student perspective and held us accountable for continuous improvement.

I hope this helps you reduce survey apathy in your organization and improve your organization overall.

"In communications, familiarity breeds apathy."—William Bernbach, American businessman

Recognition

Personalized Recognition

I am still amazed managers have not learned that all people do not like public recognition. For some people, the recognition one-size-fits all program does not work. Some employees, as well as managers, like public recognition, and some like private recognition.

While all people want to be appreciated, this takes many forms. There are several ways to handle this. In your one-on-one coaching meetings, you can ask your employees or managers what is important to them.

- Some might say public recognition in front of the team or as part of the team.
- Some might say a certificate.
- Some might say money, a gift card, a day off, a trophy.
- For others, the response might be a simple card or saying "Thank you."

Over the years, I have found recognition is unique to the person. I have read many books on this subject and want to share some fun ideas I have used for my team.

- Favorite snack for a meeting that is individualized to each person
- Favorite candy left as a surprise on the desk
- Favorite food/restaurant and gift card
- Baking a special treat that the employee likes

Other unusual things I did:

- Ordered three tickets for the children's symphony for a Saturday one of my male managers was working. The tickets were for his wife and two girls.

- Ordered flowers for the wife of one of my managers to welcome the family to Houston.
- Took the team out to do kart racing to celebrate our success.
- Invited an employee to lunch who does not directly report to me, and they were allowed to bring a colleague with them.
- Took a manager to dinner who moved to Houston prior to his family joining him. After dinner, gave him a tour of Houston to help him find neighborhoods with great schools where he and his family might want to live.
- Allowed a special training opportunity for growth and development that meant something to the individual.
- Left a special book on their desk.
- Hosted lunch and shoe-shopping as my treat to my female managers.

Did I expense this to the company? No. These were my personal ways to express my appreciation. This is not an exhaustive list but some ideas to find out what might work for your team. Finally, if you do not know, ask them.

"A job well done is the epitaph of mediocrity and the prologue of excellence."–Anonymous

Thank You—the Two Most Powerful Words in the World

It is the little things in life that make a difference. We have all heard that saying, but how do we put it into practice? Saying "Thank you" is becoming more and more a rare event. We all appreciate recognition, and it comes in many forms. Saying "Thank you" is the easiest way to make a real difference. Each session at the university, we surveyed our students to assess the teaching quality in the classroom. We had a 4.0 scale that ranged from poor to average to very good to exceptional. The faculty for our location exceeded the minimum ratings each session. Our faculty members were amazing, and the majority scored in the very good to exceptional range. Each session, I hand-wrote thank-you notes to the faculty. It was a large number of thank-you notes. For each session, I would choose thank-you notes with new designs. When I first started this, I noticed that faculty members often pinned the notes to the walls of their cubicles. Other faculty members would notice and ask about the cards and how they received a thank-you note. It became a topic of conversation and competition with the faculty.

I know they appreciated it as they would stop by my office and say "Thank you" for the thank-you note. We would laugh! It truly touched my heart that they would take the time to stop by.

Did it take time to write these? Yes. Was it worth it? Yes. It was not an email or a text. They knew each note was written especially for them.

I was consistent each session and never missed, no matter how busy I was. The next habit I got into was that each Friday, I would sit at my desk and write five to ten thank-you notes to staff or managers or faculty for doing something positive that I noticed. I also asked my managers to let me know about good things individuals or groups did, so I could send them a thank-you note. I could not always know what was happening and needed their eyes and ears. They were always proud to tell about one of their team member's accomplishments.

This small and genuine gesture made a big difference. When was the last time you wrote a thank-you note?

"People do not care about how much you know until they know how much you care."–Theodore Roosevelt, American politician and 26th US President

Lesson Learned from *This is Us*

Season 1, Episode 17 of the television series *This Is Us* was thought-provoking for me. As a leader and manager, I cannot shake the impression it left on me. *This Is Us* is a story of a modern-day, real-life family with struggles, joys, and steadfast love. In this episode, Randall's birth father, William, dies.

So how does this relate to leadership and management? Randall has worked for his company for the past ten years helping build the company into one of the most successful in its industry. He has often given twenty hours a day, missing time with family and friends, and time for himself.

His boss sent a box of pears upon hearing of the passing of his father. Randall had taken some personal time off to be with his father before his passing. A few days later, Randall went back to the office at ten at night, knowing everyone, including the boss, would be working in the board room.

Randall barged into the room and the boss looked up, happy to see Randall is ready to jump back in and help the team. Randall does not jump in. Randall asks his boss, "How could you send a box of pears when I just lost my father?" Randall said, "You have known for the past ten years that I am allergic to pears. On my first day at work, we went to lunch, and the salad I had had pears in it, and I went into anaphylactic shock. Basically, this is how you treat me?"

I have often seen insensitive gestures of this kind in business. Bosses make a gesture and do something without real thought. It really made me think. Do you know your employees and managers? Do you know what they care about? Do you make an effort? Do you know about their families? Do you have any idea about their lives? Do you know their likes, dislikes, allergies, hopes, and dreams?

About six years ago, I started a new job. Early on, I took some homemade baked goods into the office to contribute to a function. One of my employees came up to me and asked if I baked the items. I said, "Yes." He said he had just read an article that said real leaders do not bake. I laughed when I heard the title and wondered what led to writing it. I often bake for my employees in order to let them know they are valuable.

First, I like baking and feel it is a contribution from my heart. Second, I know dessert is not for everyone. I would often find out the exact treat the employee enjoyed and make that dessert for them. For some employees, sugar was on the list of foods to be avoided, so I did something else that was meaningful for them. The point is, I knew my employees. The baking was a way I could show I cared, and I did. Does baking keep me from being less of a leader? No.

While the episode on *This Is Us* was about death, the loss of a beloved father, it was also about the insensitivity of management and leaders. Get to know your employees and managers. Each person is an individual with hopes, dreams, families, and feelings. People are interesting and different. Be sensitive and show you care.

Write down all the ways you can demonstrate care of your employees and what is meaningful to each of them.

"Randall is not free of vice. His vice is his goodness."–Randall's TV wife from *This is Us*

Talent Development

Developing Talent from the Inside Out

Do you occasionally have an opening for a management position? You place the ads externally as required but do not seem to really find a person with the right set of skills? I used to play a game with myself, thinking through all the people who worked for my organization. Since I worked in a multi-story building, I would visually imagine each person working for our organization, floor by floor. I would think about what made them unique. I would think about the specific skills they offered in relation to the skills needed for the open management position. I would not think about their current position or title.

I was always committed to finding the right person for the position and building our team from within when possible.

Once I thought we had such a person on our team, I would get input from the person's manager on whether they felt the skills were a match. I would invite the manager to have a conversation with the employee to see if they had an interest in applying. It was always up to the employee and manager.

During the twenty-plus years I used this strategy, I had many supervisors shake their heads and wonder about how certain employees ended up in certain roles. Most of those supervisors thought in a linear fashion and could not think outside the box. Well, the proof is in the results. All of those employees who applied and took on the new role, often crossing departmental lines and starting anew, were incredibly successful.

My advice is never put someone in a box or a role. People are interesting and complex and have a lot to offer if you just let them. Let them shine! Once you do this, support them in their success.

"The healthiest companies are always characterized by organic talent development."–Margaret Heffernan, American businesswoman

Labels Are for Food, Not People

Have you ever been in a meeting when a manager was talking in a negative way about an employee in front of a group of other managers? Have you ever really thought about the impact of such a conversation on the person being talked about? The conversation might go something like this: "Hey, did you know that Joe . . ." This goes on to describe a mistake the manager had made. The next part of the conversation says that this manager is not promotable. From here it gets worse: the manager labels this person as ___, and Joe basically becomes a person who lives in this box and label. This manager has decided the future career of Joe all in one conversation.

I have unfortunately been a part of these types of conversations and meetings many times, but I did not remain silent. If I knew of the actual situation, I would fill in some facts that were not shared about the circumstances, or I might suggest to the team that although a mistake had been made, that what is being said is not who the person is.

I would remind the team of all the contributions this person had made to the organization. I wish I could say my comments made an impact, but at first they did not. I would then attend other meetings, where the same manager would continue to drill home the information about the mistake Joe had made.

I am sure it made the manager feel superior. It made me feel the manager was being inappropriate. What was even more interesting was that this manager did not manage Joe. It was all hearsay. For at least two more meetings, I would remind the team: yes, Joe did make a mistake, but it is not who he is. I would also remind the team we had learned a valuable lesson and needed to see it as a way to improve. This is only one example that was repeated through my organization.

In this particular situation, this organization boasted they were a learning organization. I felt compelled to remind them of who we were and what a learning organization actually means. After about three meetings, the conversation about Joe shifted, and the mistake was forgotten. Eventually, people learned not to label people around me. Later, Joe went on to be promoted, and he contributed a great deal to the organization. How many times has someone labeled someone else in an organization and doomed their career?

Labels are not for people; labels are for food products.

"Don't let anyone label you. People are not jars, but they can break easily."–Unknown

What Do You Mean, I Am Not Getting the Promotion?

As a matter of procedure, most organizations post openings internally before the position openings are posted externally. This gives internal candidates time to think about the new opportunity, the skill set needed, and whether to apply. I really like this procedure, to allow the internal team members new opportunities for growth and promotion. It is a good way to build bench strength.

Having said that, what happens when you have one position opening and you have three internal candidates apply? Obviously, only one person can be selected, and there is no guarantee it will be an internal candidate. Most organizations hope the opening can be filled by an internal candidate if the skill set is a match. The internal candidate knows the culture, the mission, and vision, and ideally will make an easier transition.

In reality, I have often found that internal candidates do not have a good self-awareness about themselves at work. What usually happens is the internal candidate(s) come in one at a time. They are dressed professionally. They have brought multiple copies of their resumes. They have a PowerPoint presentation to discuss how they meet the skills required for the job. The dialogue goes well. It is usually quite impressive. The candidate thanks everyone and leaves the room.

The interview panel scores the interview form and then the discussion about the candidate takes place. For many of the candidates, the conversation that follows does not go well. While the interview was sensational, the panel starts to look at the candidate's current job performance in their current role. There may be certain known facts about the employee's past performance such as:

- The candidate may not arrive on time to work.
- The candidate may not dress professionally.
- The candidate might cause drama at work and so on . . . you get the idea.

Once a final decision has been made, I strongly believe Human Resources or the hiring manager should explain to all candidates, especially internal candidates, why they were not selected.

We know the internal candidates will be disappointed to learn they were not selected. I believe it is our job to be candid so they can do a better job in their current role and have a better chance at the next internal opportunity. We are not saying they will never be promoted. We are just saying not now.

What I always say to internal candidates is that you have to be twice as good as the external candidate. They look at me with surprise. I explain that we know who they are. We have seen them operate for the last two years or more. I explain that while the interview was impressive, they did not demonstrate that level of professionalism each day. I further explain if they really want a promotion, they should do every day what they did in the interview, and they will get noticed. They will grow and become a better contributor.

Trust me, this not what they want to hear, but given time, they always come back to me and thank me for being candid, as they know I want them to succeed.

"If you want a promotion, you must find the courage and confidence to promote yourself."–Anonymous

Talent Development / Leadership Academy

Employees are our greatest resource. It has always been that way, whether the organization was willing to admit it or not. In today's workforce, it is even more important. Our workforce mix is changing, and soon the millennial population will be the majority while other generations diminish through retirement, etc.

What is most important to our employees is the opportunity to grow, contribute, and advance. While organizations are struggling to balance salaries, benefits, and profits; and be the best place to work, there is one thing that can help: investing in our people. It is the job of every manager and leader. Your first response to this statement might be that this is a Human Resources job, but think again.

You are responsible for your team. While it would be great to partner with Human Resources and senior leadership, you can certainly get the idea started. I have found that building an internal leadership academy is very effective. With all the great technology available, learning management systems (LMS), and internal talent, you can build one, too. It really does not require a lot of capital resources, just time and effort.

So we start with the end in mind. What do we want to accomplish with a leadership or professional development academy? Who should participate? What are the learning outcomes? What topics support the learning outcomes? How long should the course be? What is the best delivery modality?

Think about your mission. Incorporate the tools you have in your organization to help employees, such as developing an individual development plan. From there, teach them about the overall operation. There is no guarantee of advancement, but each employee will gain a broader understanding of the operation. This will build their confidence. They can serve your clients more effectively. Eventually, they will be ready to take on more. Provide an internal mentor. Create a structure for success that includes a syllabus, timeline, and a way to measure the results. Have senior leadership help facilitate the modules.

Include employees from all parts of the organization. Evaluate at the end of the academy. What worked? What needs to be changed?

Over time, you will be amazed at what happens. An investment in your employees is priceless.

"Your talent determines what you can do. Your motivation determines what you are willing to do. Your attitude determines how well you will do it."–Lou Holtz, Football player and coach

To Train or Not to Train–Face-To-Face Training for Specialty Positions

I am often amused by management's lack of understanding of the value of training and the return on investment (ROI). Often organizations decide they need to fill a certain role, whether it is at one location or multiple locations. They post the position and get the person started. Sometimes they provide webinar-type training, policies and procedures, and even a portal for electronic resources. The company thinks they have done everything to have the person be successful. Think again.

I am a big proponent of webinar training for all the obvious reasons, such as reduced costs, travel time, and expenses; a larger global audience can be reached, etc. The training can be recorded and delivered any time, any place. I use it myself, but not in the beginning. In the beginning, we need a high-touch–then high-tech–approach.

About twelve years ago, I was very fortunate to work for a company that listened to me about how I wanted things to go in hiring for a specialty position at our locations. Fortunately for me, all these positions were not filled on the same day.

I wanted our new employees or newly designated employees to know they had corporate support, which started with an initial three-day, face-to-face training. I would travel to their location and train them for three days. I would introduce them to the resources. I would show them a plan for the initial year and modify it, based on their location and team. I would listen to what they wanted to bring to the position. During the three days, we would include role-playing and presenting materials. Initially, it was a lot of work, but it paid off in the long run in so many ways.

First, the new employee felt supported. Second, they knew where to access information. Third, we got to know each other as we were sitting side by side. The connection was always strong. After the initial training, we moved to a schedule of conference calls, monthly webinars, and train-the-trainer sessions as a group, etc. They felt comfortable in asking questions or sharing what was working or what was not working. It was safe.

While there were costs for me to travel, the return on the investment was evident. The quality of the work of the new employee was excellent, which impacted so many. It was consistent. The point is that I did not phone it in and say to our new employees, "Just call me if you need anything." I modeled what I expected, and they in turn did the same. Try it, and see if the ROI is greater than expected.

"You don't have to be great to start; you have to start to be great."
–Zig Ziglar, speaker and author

Mind, Body, and Spirit

The one thing I know for sure is that you cannot lead, manage, and inspire without feeling your very best. It is part of your responsibility to care of yourself and to model for others. There are certainly many ways to incorporate all three.

As a leader, it is imperative you are current on the latest trends and topics. You can do this by reading, listening to audio books or podcasts, conducting research, taking classes, participating in webinars, etc. Whatever your preference is, you need to routinely feed your mind with new information outside of your work environment. Some of the best ideas come from other sources outside your organization that inform your thinking in new ways.

For your body, choose something you enjoy doing, and do it habitually. This could be walking ten thousand steps a day, working out, yoga, swimming, biking, running, hiking, dancing, martial arts, playing organized sports, or doing other activities. Whatever you choose, enjoy it, or you will not stay with it. Your mind and your body will thank you. People in your organization and your family are counting on the fact you will take care of yourself, because they know stress is a large part of the job. It is really not healthy to be out of breath going up one flight of stairs when you are giving a tour, for example.

Another part of this is nutrition. Take care of your body so you have enough energy to lead and manage. Over-indulging in anything is not good. American health issues are very serious. These chronic conditions, such as obesity, contribute to the healthcare crisis as well as the costs.

Finally, feed your spirit. This can be attending a formal religious service or church that feeds your soul. It can be meditating, visiting a place sacred to you, praying, or however you express yourself to the spirit. It is time to reflect and be grateful for all you have been given.

All of these are important aspects to taking care of the whole you, so you can give one hundred percent when you are leading or managing. Celebrate your mind, body, and spirit, and be an inspiration to your team and someone they want to follow.

"The body heals with play, the mind heals with laughter, and the spirit heals with joy."—proverb

Defining Moments

There will be defining moments in your career when you are confronted with a situation that determines the next steps in your career. Be listening for those opportunities to demonstrate success.

Looking back at my career, I see that there were defining moments all along the way. For example, I worked for a university for about a three-month period. It was the fall semester, and I noticed a number of new teachers did not know the proper protocol. After I finished teaching my class, I went to visit with the Dean of Education. I mentioned what I had seen and suggested the university provide a new-employee orientation. He said that it was a good idea, and told me I should do that.

I knew the components for delivering an effective orientation, yet there were areas of the university I did not know. I knew I needed to partner with someone who knew all the people at the university and had been on every floor. So I thought about my previous experience in the hospitality industry. The most knowledgeable people in a hotel are members of the bell staff. They meet every guest. They have been in every room. They hear all the comments. They have to describe all the amenities offered at the hotel. I needed someone like a bellman. So who would that be at a university?

I discovered my best asset would the director of Readmissions. The director of Readmissions works with students who have withdrawn from the university. It takes a special person to perform this role. You have to be great with establishing relationships and be an expert in programs and resources.

I decided to partner with another colleague named Cliff, who was the Readmissions staff member and had been at the university for many years. He was trusted and knowledgeable and a delight to work with. Diligently, we offered a new-employee orientation. Each quarter, it improved.

Another time, my supervisor asked me to create a faculty development program for his faculty. I had never done anything like it before but said yes. I had the skill set but not the actual experience yet.

We had it approved by the certifying agency, and then I taught all of his faculty. Ten years later, these two projects turned into my obtaining the career of my dreams as vice president of Faculty Development for the university company. If at any point I had just complained about no employee orientation or whatever the problem was at work and not been part of the solution, my career would have turned out differently.

Look around and see people at work where their careers are stagnant, then pay attention to what they say at work or if they complain. There is no coincidence. I have many more examples of when I was confronted with a problem or listened to people complain about a situation at work. I immediately went to creating a solution or saying yes to help someone solve a problem. It certainly reduced my frustrations and actually provided fulfillment for me personally.

Listen for the problems, but be part of the solution and not the company complaint crowd. You will be amazed at what happens next. Your attitude makes all the difference. Decide if you want to be part of the problem or part of the solution. Look for those defining moments. They are all around you. What have been your defining moments?

"A lot of people failed at what you accomplished, simply because they were busy finding problems while you were busy finding solutions." –Anonymous

I Have a Problem

Have you ever had an employee come by your office and tell you they have a problem? Or they say, "We have a problem," meaning "you?" If you are a new manager, you may feel you have to solve all the problems and provide all the answers. Do you really think that helps? If you start this bad habit, you will never get your work done, and you are not helping the situation or the person.

What is your role as manager? It is to help employees grow and learn and solve problems. Your job as a manager is to listen fully to what the employee is saying. They are probably bringing you gold. After listening intently, I would usually ask the employee, "How would you propose we solve this problem?" They would think for a minute and usually had a great approach.

I think sometimes employees feel they need to bring problems to the manager to solve. This approach does not help anyone or the organization. Half of this approach is correct. The employee should feel comfortable bringing an issue or problem to the manager. But the manager should help the employee think through how the employee should solve the problem.

What you want to do is to teach the employee that when they bring you a problem, they need to have thought about a possible solution or approach. You can do this in a respectful way, so over time they learn how to solve the problem, and not end up leaving it on your desk to solve.

We hope they will want to advance in their career; problem-solving is a skill set they will need to learn. Let's help them build critical-thinking skills, communication skills, and enhance problem-solving skills. What strategies have you used and found to be effective?

"Be part of the solution and answer the problem versus part of the problem and continuing argument around it."–David Pratt, Christian author

Time Management

Balancing Life on a Seesaw

I have never understood the concept of work-life balance. I have been working for forty years, and this concept does not make sense to me. It is not realistic. On one hand, it seems like it is something for which we should strive, but it seems to me more like a guilt trip if we do not do this.

Life is like a seesaw. Sometimes we are up and sometimes we are down, and sometimes life is balanced or in the middle. My thinking is that when we are up, we have a lot of things going on both at work and family. We are in the zone. There is high energy and momentum. It is exciting, and we can handle all of it. The truth is that sometimes when we are up at work, certain areas of our life require more attention, such as work or family. It is not equal. It can be stressful at the same time. Being up all of the time is not sustainable.

When we are on the bottom, at that resting state, it is more like we are stuck. Not much is going on. We might have just completed a large project at work or a family event or celebration, and we feel dead. There is no activity. No momentum. At this point, you need to determine how to get back up.

Being in the middle of the seesaw, the balanced position, is a key time. It is not splitting work and family life fifty-fifty. It is time to take care of yourself. It is time to take time out of each day for reflection and creativity. Self-care might be yoga, walking, painting, writing, working out, getting a massage, or taking a bath–anything that allows you time to think and create a new way to move the seesaw and enjoy your life to the fullest. When was the last time you were on a seesaw? Notice the children's faces next time you are at the park. They are fully self-expressed. When was the last time you felt that way?

"Balance–never let success go to your head, and never let failure go to your heart."–Natural Life by LifeQuotes.com

Weekly Habits

One of the best habits I developed over time is a ritual at the end of each week. For me, it is best to do this on Friday afternoon or Saturday morning, depending on what is scheduled at work. I carve out some downtime at the office and began preparing for the upcoming week. I look at my calendar for each day of the next week. I lay out the calendar day by day and examine what I am accountable for, such as meetings, trainings, conference calls, etc. I print out each calendar day and place it into a colored folder. The folders are labeled Monday through Saturday, as we have a lot of events held on Saturday. You do not have to print anything out like I did, but it helped me think through what I needed.

An electronic filing system like One Note is ideal. See http://www.onenote.com/ for instructions on how to use the efficient system, which comes with Microsoft Office Suite.

For every event I was accountable for, I created the agenda, handouts, or reports I needed. I placed the items in the folder for that day, in chronological order. I did this for each day of the upcoming week. It saved so much time for the next week. We all know that sometimes we have meetings that run over or unexpected calls, and we are rushing. I never had to worry about looking for a report making me late to the next meeting, as it was in the folder. I did not waste time, and I set a good example.

When I left work on Friday night or Saturday, I actually could relax instead of worrying about the next week. Too many times, managers keep details floating around in their heads. That takes away from their being present with family, causing undue stress.

So when I returned to work, I was ready. At the end of each of workday, I would look at the next day to update anything I needed for that day. As we know, items would be added and deleted, so I needed to be current. Once you get into this habit, you will be less stressed and honestly much more creative at work. Repeat each Friday or Saturday. You will be amazed about how productive you become and how great you feel.

Are you stressed at times? How present are you at work or with family? Try this, and see if it improves the quality of your life. What weekly habits have you developed?

"You'll never change your life until you change something you do daily. The secret of your success is found in your daily routine." –John Maxwell, American author, speaker, and pastor

Just Schedule It!

Have you ever noticed how disorganized some leaders and managers are? Have you ever wondered how it is the business continues? Or if you are the leader, do you ever wonder how time flies and all of a sudden Quarter One is about over and you did not accomplish certain things?

Once you are firmly grounded in your position and know what you want to accomplish, schedule it. I have found that by scheduling the year out in advance, we are prone to fewer surprises. So what do I mean by that? I am not talking about scheduling every detail. I am talking about the large, recurring events you and your organization feel are important. For example, weekly Executive Committee meetings, weekly sales meetings, monthly town-hall meetings, quarterly operational and planning meetings, quarterly marketing meetings, annual SWOT meetings, annual strategic-planning meetings, budgeting week meetings, annual reviews, safety meetings, standing meetings, orientations, company campaigns, training days, holidays, holiday picnics or parties, etc.

Map out the meetings you know you want to hold, and then schedule the date, time, and length of the meeting. Now you have a placeholder and can share the calendar with your team. From this, you create an event calendar that can be written in a Word document and added to a SharePoint site, calendar, or the company portal. You can also invite the meeting participants through the use of Microsoft Outlook calendars. Update as necessary.

This makes it easier on everyone to plan and be prepared. Your employees can also schedule vacations or time off around the events when they know in advance what is occurring.

This may seem like overkill to some employees and managers, but I have found it reduces stress for everyone, and employees respect this approach. What areas can you schedule more effectively?

"If you talk about it, it's just a dream; if you envision it, it's possible; but if you schedule it, it's real."–Anthony Robbins, author, actor, and professional speaker

Conclusion

This book is intended as one simple, practical tool to be used week by week. As you try each idea, take a few minutes to make notes on what worked, the feedback you received from the team, and what could be improved at your organization. It is based on years of trial and error in what worked and what did not work for me personally. The intention of this book is:

- To save you time
- To make a larger impact
- To build strong relationships with your team and organization
- To provide a more logical approach

Weaving in one strategy each week, making notes, and reflecting will help each member of the management and leadership team enhance their own effectiveness over the course of the year. The goal is to take a new strategy each week and by the end of the year, have a much more confident leader with a new set of practical tools.

Wishing you and your team the opportunity to experience exceptional leadership!

www.ingramcontent.com/pod-product-compliance
Lightning Source LLC
Chambersburg PA
CBHW052013230326
41598CB00078B/3215

* 9 7 8 1 6 2 7 4 7 1 7 4 9 *